Praise for *Work. Pump. Repeat.*
How to Survive Breastfeeding and Going Back to Work

I read *Work. Pump. Repeat.* both as a mother who breastfed and worked, and as an IBCLC. The information in this book is spot-on regarding the science behind lactation . . . written so that stressed working moms will understand it with no jargon to wade through. Ms. Shortall tells it like it is and doesn't sugarcoat the realities of breastfeeding and working.

Robyn Roche-Paull, BSN, RN, IBCLC,
author of *Breastfeeding in Combat Boots: A Survival Guide to Successful Breastfeeding While Serving in the Military*

. . . you feel as if your wicked smart and big-hearted friend sat you down to give you the good, the bad and the often hilarious reality about pumping at work. Jessica makes sense of the science, simplifies the mechanics, and balances practicalities with personal stories that disarm the mom guilt. You can't help but laugh your way through as she covers the details that other books fail to include. Finally a comprehensive book on pumping at work I feel confident about recommending to my clients!

Elaine McGhee, founder, ThriveMomma.com

Where the hell was this book five years ago when I needed it!? Jessica manages to be both hilarious and informative in the non-condescending manner that can only come from someone who has truly been there. I described this book to a friend as "postpartum-pee-inducing funny." It is a book I want to buy not only for my soon-to-be-working-mom friends, but also for all of my co-workers so that they can just finally understand.

Chelsea Nelson, Liberating Working Moms

A must-read for any mom who plans to pump at work. Jessica Shortall provides a thorough, practical, and relatable guide to the many challenges and rewards of being a pumping mom. She nimbly avoids controversy and judgment and presents all the things a working mom needs to know, even the things she didn't know she needs to know.

JJ Keith, author of *Motherhood Smotherhood*

... a solid advice guide that should be on the shelves of any woman who enjoys a career and who wants to return to it while continuing to nurture her child: a guide very highly recommended for its exceptional focus and well-rounded discussion of the realities of the venture.

D. Donovan, Senior eBook Reviewer,
Midwest Book Review

As IBCLCs, we understand the theory behind pumping and the production of breast milk. However, no one can understand the practicalities and the emotional cost better than a mom who has done it! Jessica Shortall's book has hit on an area of need. Based on her own experience, she delivers practical how-to's that other books are missing.

Cindy Leclerc, RN IBCLC & Jana Stockham, RN IBCLC,
co-creators of NuuNest

WORK.
PUMP.
REPEAT.

How to Survive Breastfeeding and Going Back to Work

Jessica Shortall

Otet Press

Dallas

Work. Pump. Repeat.
How to Survive Breastfeeding and Going Back to Work

Copyright © 2014 Jessica Jackson Shortall.

All rights reserved. No part of this book may be used or reproduced by any means, graphic, electronic, or mechanical, including photocopying, recording, taping, or by any information storage retrieval system without the written permission of the publisher, except in the case of brief quotations embodied in critical articles and reviews.

Books may be ordered through booksellers or by contacting:

Otet Press
P.O. Box 180882
Dallas, TX 75218
USA

www.workpumprepeat.com

Because of the dynamic nature of the Internet, any web addresses or links contained in this book may have changed since publication and may no longer be valid.

The views expressed in this work are solely those of the author.

Cover design by Bee Things
Author photo by Laura Legg Photography

ISBN: 978-0-9909192-0-9 (sc)
ISBN: 978-0-9909192-1-6 (e)

Printed in the United States of America

This book is dedicated to every woman who has ever sat on a public toilet with a breast pump balanced on her knees.

Acknowledgements

I call this book my love letter to working mothers. But the process of writing this book has in many ways been a love letter to *me*, from friends and strangers who have made this project possible.

Thank you to the working mothers and HR professionals who made the time to share your wisdom and war stories.

Thank you to my beloved TOMS co-workers for letting me disappear into storage closets, leave meetings early, pump on conference calls, and store milk in the office freezer. I never doubted that you supported me in providing for my kids. Thanks also for asking just enough, and not too many, weird questions about breastfeeding.

Thank you to Candice Kislack, my lifeline on an epic journey to Nepal. Everyone should have a boss and friend like you.

Thank you to Karen Borchert and Kate Canales for believing in this book way before it was a book, and for being, along with my sister Ianthé, the people I text whenever something astonishing related to motherhood happens.

Thank you to every connector, cheerleader, blogger, and promoter who has championed this book. You are too numerous to name, but I appreciate the hell out of each of you.

Thank you to this book's many benefactors, including Elena Davis, Bob Gutermuth and Greg Durham, Justin Wong, and Liz Taylor.

Thank you to my editors: Tiffany Gallagher, CLC (a.k.a. The Boob Geek), who was both copyeditor and technical advisor, and whose input made this book so much better; and Sue Toth, who let me keep my Oxford Comma. And God bless my volunteer readers, who worked wonders: Taylor Skinner, Karen Borchert, Jenny Magic, Erin Olson, and Tiffany Galligan.

Thank you to the breastfeeding experts who cast discerning eyes on the manuscript: Robyn Roche-Paull, BSN, RN, IBCLC; Cindy Leclerc RN, IBCLC; and Jana Stockham RN, IBCLC.

Thank you to Shay Ometz and Jeff Barfoot of Bee Things, for using your formidable cover design skills for a book about boobs.

Thank you to my family (wonderful in-laws very much included). It will never stop amazing me that all of you so unflinchingly support every eclectic dream I pursue. Special thanks to my husband Clay, who has believed in this book and every other endeavor I've undertaken, and my children, Otis and Etta, who make life magical by solemnly giving me autumn leaves and disembodied Lego heads as gifts.

Finally, thank you to every airport TSA agent who has waved me through security without dismantling my pump or opening my milk to test it. You are the real heroes.

Contents

Introduction 1

Section 1: Preparation

1: The Basics of Making Milk 13
2: Meet Your Pump 17
3: Pumping School 27
4: Bottles and Freezer Stash 33
5: Clothing 53
6: Breastfeeding Rights at Work 59

Section 2: On the Job

7: What You'll Need at Work 69
8: Making a Plan Your Boss Will Like 81
9: Time, Privacy, and Awkward Co-Workers 109
10: Washing and Storing 125
11: Pumping in Strange Places 129

Section 3: Business Travel

12: Doing Your Business on a Business Trip 151

13: The Mile-High Milk Club 159

14: Traveling with Your Baby 173

Section 4: Problem Solving

15: Supply and Supplementing 183

16: Weaning 195

17: Surviving Disaster Days 209

18: Stress and Guilt 231

19: Resources 243

WORK.
PUMP.
REPEAT.

Introduction

Here's an idea: Pretty soon after we have babies, let's use machines to extract breastmilk from our bodies several times a day while we are working demanding jobs. Let's do this when we are already exhausted, anxious, stressed, and overwhelmed—and trying to prove to our employers that we're "back."

Who on Earth would do this? Well, for starters:

- A police officer: "I pumped in the car at a site where I was helping to recover the skeleton of a murder victim from a creek bed."
- A teacher: "I've been walked in on twice, despite displaying do-not-disturb signs. Both were male. One backed away slowly. The other stayed to chat."
- A communications director: "I'm limited to thirty-minute pumping sessions, so I often have to leave in the middle of an hour-long meeting and call in for the remainder."
- A doctor at a hospital: "I had to pump while answering pages, talking on the phone, or eating lunch. Once, I forgot my bottles and had to pump into urine collection cups. I swear they were sterile."

...and me. I'm a working mother of two, and when I had my first baby, working and breastfeeding became one of the most difficult experiences of my professional life.

Continuing to breastfeed after I returned to work was something I really wanted to do. But it also produced more anxiety and guilt and feelings of being overwhelmed than any other part of parenting. It was a very physical job in the midst of an already physically trying time in my life—the lugging of equipment and milk, the running between meetings and pumping sessions, and the finding of private places in which to pump.

It was also an emotional job, filled with second guesses. It was time-consuming, draining (literally), anxiety-producing, and stressful. Being someone's sole (or main) source of nutrition is hard work.

It was rewarding, too, and I did it as best as I could. I was the first woman to have a baby at my company, so I had no precedent and no mentors at the office. I did about a dozen domestic and international business trips during the nine months I breastfed my son. I pumped in storage closets and on airplanes and in far-flung locations in developing countries. I fought TSA agents over my frozen milk. I stared at photos of my son while pumping, trying to force my body to produce just a little more milk. I spilled tears onto those same photos. I also brought that milk home with a sense of pride and relief every day.

I counted every single ounce I made and stressed about my son "beating" me by eating more than I had pumped in a given day. I did all of this for nine months, and then I woke up one day and just knew there was no more gas left in the tank. So I stopped.

The hows of working and breastfeeding are many, and can be overwhelming and confusing. How to build up a stash of milk, how to find work-appropriate clothes you can pump in, how to talk to your boss about your needs, how to commandeer and hack virtually any space to pump in. A huge pile of hows that no one ever bothered to jot down for us "triple threat" mothers (worker/parent/milk-maker).

In a world overflowing with more parenting books and Pinterest sites and mommy blogs than you can shake a positive pregnancy stick at, why is the Motherhood Industrial Complex failing us when it comes to breastfeeding in the working world? There are stacks and stacks of books to tell us how to get pregnant, be pregnant, birth a baby, nurse a baby, sleep train a baby, follow its development on a moment-by-moment basis, and raise a child. These books are overflowing with opinions (often conflicting) on the right and wrong ways to do all of these things.

But many of these same books gloss over how hard breastfeeding is. And working and breastfeeding? That gets a paragraph, if you're lucky. Just look at the covers of most breastfeeding books and you'll see a drawing of a mother, still in her bathrobe, cuddling her baby at her breast. For working mothers, that image might work in the first couple of weeks (especially the bathrobe part), but the long-term reality looks more like stirring a pot of food while on a conference call while trying to breastfeed a baby while kicking (gently! lovingly!) at a toddler to get out of the kitchen. This makes for a busy book cover, but it's the truth.

I think a big driver of this problem is that so much of breastfeeding education is focused on those early days and weeks, when breastfeeding is often confusing, painful, and exhausting.

The relatively new phenomenon of lots of women heading off to work with breast pumps in tow is just not covered in the same way by the breastfeeding literature. Many breastfeeding professionals I interviewed shared that pumping at work is an underserved area for the lactation community, and that was a major motivation for me to write this book.

What You'll Find in This Book

For me, other working mothers have been the only source for practical, honest, and funny information about how to breastfeed and work. Only they have the war stories and the insightful insider tricks. Only they truly get the guilt, pressure, and anxiety that breastfeeding and work can add to the already stressful situation of going back to work. And only they can laugh about the whole thing, when nobody else in the world seems to find any of this even remotely funny.

So, what I offer you, modern mama with too much on your plate, is a straight-to-the-point resource that will complement the essential breastfeeding stuff that's already out there.

I'm not going to tell you about football hold or proper latch or give you a cookie recipe to increase your milk—all of that exists, and you really ought to read it. What I will give you, because I couldn't find these things anywhere else myself, are as follows:

- Practical tools for the situations working, breastfeeding mothers find themselves in: the gear, the tricks to navigate the workplace, the coping strategies.
- Insight into your rights and responsibilities at work, and advice on how to approach your employer on this subject.
- Stories from other working moms to make you laugh, cry, or cringe (maybe all three); to help you navigate your situation; and to remind you that you're not alone.
- Tactics to balance a busy schedule with the demands of pumping.
- Honest, non-judgmental support for the feelings of anxiety and pressure that are so common to working breastfeeders.

This advice comes straight to you from my own experiences and the experiences of hundreds of other working mothers—plus some HR professionals for additional perspective.

In writing this book, I took working mothers out to lunch; talked to them over the phone, email, and Skype; and asked the question, "What was breastfeeding and working like for you?"

They cried; I cried. We laughed, and peed our pants a little, in true just-had-a-baby style. Many told me that breastfeeding was, for all of its ups and downs, a really positive experience. They were amazed at what their bodies could do. They loved that they could still do something for their babies when they were at work. And they treasured reconnecting with their babies when they got home from a long day or a long trip.

I felt honored that they would share their stories with me. In this book, you will find the collective wisdom of these women.

These women are practical. They are goal-oriented. They've worked hard to try to provide their babies with breastmilk. Some have done it for months or years, others for days or weeks.

Most of these women struggled with breastfeeding and working, but almost all felt pride at giving it their best shot. They all deserve a medal in the form of a beverage of their choice and a solid hour when nobody is allowed to touch them or talk to them.

Only these fellow working mothers can remind you to buy multiple sets of pumping parts for the days when you forget one piece and end up pumping into Ziploc bags or coffee cups (which you can steam-sterilize in the office microwave!).

They know the importance of back-up clothes in a desk drawer or filing cabinet, for when you leak breastmilk all over your blouse.

They can tell you about handling pressure from co-workers—including, amazingly, HR and other women—to stop pumping.

They know what it's like to be walked in on while hooked up to a breast pump, by a firm partner, the company CEO, a client, or the Harlem Globetrotters (seriously).

They know what to say to the security agent at the airport who wants to open a bag of breastmilk on the way home from a business trip.

And they can tell you exactly how to pump in a moving car or on an airplane or in a storage closet with no lock.

Here's the truth: We're all inventing solutions as we go. We all doubt ourselves and wonder if we're coming up short. But we're smart and we're good at solving problems, and by collecting our solutions in one place, we can help countless new mothers do this difficult job as painlessly as possible.

Breastfeeding while working is not easy, and I don't know if you'll meet a working mother who will tell you differently. But you can do it, and this book is here to help.

This Is a No-Judgment Zone

My assumption in writing this book is that you love your kid, and you are putting a lot of effort and energy into learning as much as you can about being a new mother. And mama, that's good enough. My mantra, which took me a long time to believe myself, is this: *your worth as a mother is not measured in ounces.*

If you're holding this book, I am guessing two things are true. First, you have already heard and absorbed a lot about the benefits of breastmilk, to your baby and to you. Second, you are informed about the differences between breastmilk and formula. It's not my job to convince you of anything. I'm here to meet you where you are.

You will not find judgment in the pages of this book (except of jerks who are rude to you about pumping or who try to milk-shame you for your feeding choices), but I do hope you find validation in your efforts to strike the elusive balance of work and motherhood. Breastfeed or don't. Do it for a week or two years. Whatever you choose, you are the best mother your baby could ask for, period.

Getting Support

I have read many breastfeeding books and I owe them a debt of gratitude for helping me figure out the mechanics of nursing a newborn. Titles like *The Womanly Art of Breastfeeding* and *The Nursing Mother's Companion* are goldmines when it comes to latching, engorgement, supply, holds, positions, and troubleshooting common problems. I recommend having one or two of these books on hand.

I similarly benefited a great deal from "live" sources of information. Prenatal breastfeeding classes can take some of the mystery out of the process, even if it means having to hold a dingy Cabbage Patch Kid to your chest in front of complete strangers.

I am not a lactation or medical professional. When you need medical advice, or you need to learn how to breastfeed in the first place, go to the experts.

Throughout this book, I will use the term "lactation professional" as a catch-all for all kinds of breastfeeding coaches. There is a wide range of professionals and volunteers available to you. In Chapter 19, you'll find a great overview, written by a lactation consultant, on the different kinds of lactation support.

Introduction

There's a lot of expert help out there, and this book will never replace those experts. Seek out the people and resources that work for you, your life, and your approach to breastfeeding. Walk away from the people and resources that do not honor your needs and your approaches to parenting and to breastfeeding.

But when you need to know how to get through a long workday without having to wash your pump parts, I'm your girl. I'm overjoyed at being able to share with you what hundreds of women have already learned about breastfeeding and work.

You're not going to be perfect, because no one ever is, but I hope that by the time you reach the end of this book, you feel educated, empowered, and supported to give it your best shot.

Notes on Style

This book is for all parents: single and divorced, married and unmarried, opposite- and same-sex. In talking about the parent who is not doing the breastfeeding, the use of words like "spouse" and "he/him" came down to simplicity and flow and is not meant to exclude any parents or family structures.

Section 1: Preparation

Before you go back to work, you can calm a lot of your anxiety and get ahead of the game. This is a nuts-and-bolts section to get you up to speed with the mechanics of pumping, give you shopping lists of the gear and clothes you'll need, help you build a milk stash at home, and equip you with the basics about your legal rights. If you can, read this section while you're pregnant or on maternity leave so you have a good head start. Get these basics down, and in Sections 2 through 4, we'll move on to the practicalities of working and breastfeeding, where you'll hear from the working moms whose wisdom is the backbone of this book.

Chapter 1: The Basics of Making Milk

Supply and Demand

In a nutshell: Producing milk is all about supply and demand. You have to demand milk from your body every day for it to keep on making milk. And give or take a bit, you have to demand the amount of milk your baby needs every day in order for your body to keep producing the volume of milk that baby needs.

As I'll say again and again: rely on at least one of the standard breastfeeding books and any number of breastfeeding websites (see Chapter 19 for a list of resources) as a necessary part of your arsenal. These resources can teach you about latching, positioning, clogged ducts, mastitis, and more. This is important stuff. I will not attempt to do the job of those resources, but as we learn about the dance of working and breastfeeding, I do think it's useful to provide a little bit of the basics on milk-making.

Your baby demands milk from your body by sucking and compressing your breasts, and your body (for most women) responds by producing milk. Not only that, but as your baby begins to demand more milk—by sucking harder, longer, and/or more frequently—your body reads those messages, too, and produces more milk over time.

This increased-supply-and-demand thing doesn't happen instantaneously; it's a gradual process. Sometimes you'll notice that your baby is doing it—like during a two-day growth-spurt where you feel like all you are doing is nursing the little vampire—and sometimes you won't, but it's still happening behind the scenes. Before you go back to work, if you aren't pumping much, you might not even know it's happened at all because you can't see how much your baby is eating at any given feeding.

Just like increased demand can lead to increased supply, a drop in demand can, over time, reduce your supply of milk. Sometimes the baby does this himself—he goes on a nursing strike, he gets sick, or he is simply taking fewer ounces of milk for each feeding as he begins to eat solid food. In these cases, as he gets interested in eating again, or recovers from his illness, he will start to demand more milk from your body, and your supply is likely to go up again. (Other factors can reduce supply, too, like being stressed, taking certain medications like decongestants or hormonal birth control, or getting sick yourself.)

For the working mother, the other culprit that can harm supply is working itself. There are many ways that work can reduce supply over time. For example, some women's bodies do not respond as well to pumping as they do to nursing a baby, so you might produce less milk during the workday than your baby is eating at home. Over time, that might lessen your overall supply.

Some women do find success with exclusive pumping (EP), which means providing breastmilk only by pumping, and not by nursing the baby. Some women EP because of persistent latch, tongue tie, or cleft palate problems, or because they like it better, or because the discipline of pumping actually helps them set goals and maintain supply.

Even if pumping does produce a good amount of milk for you in a given session, the demands of work can affect supply. If you consistently can't get in as many pumping sessions per workday as your child is having feeding sessions with his caregiver, you might see a gradual decrease in supply.

Making Sense of Supply

All of this sounds like a total nightmare to a new mother planning a return to work. It's a lot to take in and a lot to try to accomplish on top of keeping a new baby alive, worrying about your nanny or daycare or mother-in-law keeping your baby alive, being presentable for work every morning, doing your job extra well to prove to your boss that you haven't lost it as a result of having a baby, and balancing a new budget that includes hefty kid-related line items. It's stressful to feel like you have to stay on top of your milk supply, that precious resource you are trying so hard to keep flowing for your baby.

The first thing I want to say about supply stress is that I'm sorry. I have been there, as have millions of other working mothers. And we agree that, like your trusty breast pump, supply stress, well, sucks.

The second thing I will say is that establishing breastfeeding early is the best thing you can do to set yourself up for success. If breastfeeding is important to you, put in the time early on to see dividends later.

Ann, a consultant, noted, "I was successful at breastfeeding and working—nineteen months with the first child and I'm still breastfeeding a seven-month-old—because I was able to strongly establish nursing patterns before going back to work."

Finally, I want to note that this supply-and-demand thing is pretty resilient. For the vast majority of women who are able to establish a decent supply of milk during the first couple of months of the baby's life, a bad day or two is not going to permanently destroy supply.

If you have a couple of days at work that are so back-to-back that you can't pump more than once, you can bounce back from it. If you go on a business trip and find yourself producing less milk even when you are fitting lots of pumping sessions in, you can bounce back from it. Just like supply gets built up over time, it is lost over time—not overnight.

At some point, you are going to find yourself sitting in a lactation room or a supply closet or your car or an airport bathroom, staring at your two pump bottles with half an ounce of milk in them, when you're used to producing two, or even five (some over-producers go even higher) ounces per session.

You are going to look at those stupid not-full-enough bottles and think, "This is it. I've ruined my supply and I'm not going to be able to do this and I'm a horrible mother . . ." and on and on. Believe me: one bad pumping session, one bad day, one bad business trip, will not ruin your milk supply.

Chapter 2: Meet Your Pump

Your Pump: Freedom and Burden

Working motherhood has long involved a trade-off that is painful for many: breastfeed or go back to work. Today, many working mothers have a third choice: go back to work and bring your breast pump along with you.

This technology is liberating: we can work (most of us have to for financial reasons; some of us also want to because we love it) and continue to provide breastmilk for our babies.

We can also feel trapped: because the technology exists, many of us feel we have no choice but to use it, no matter how difficult, stressful, and awkward the process might be. Often both dynamics—liberation and burden—are at work at the same time.

For example: When my son was five months old, I had to go to Nepal on a business trip. Even planning for the minimum possible time on the ground (less than four days), with travel that had me circumnavigating the globe, I was going to be gone for a whole seven days. Liberation! My pump was going to allow me to do this!

Getting on a pumping schedule early on by pumping immediately after the morning feeding while I was still on leave meant that by the time this trip came around I had almost 300 ounces of breastmilk in my freezer. (I recognize that this a lot of milk, and I really stressed myself out stockpiling it. I realize in hindsight that a little formula while I was gone wouldn't have killed the kid.) In a world without breast pumps, I would have had two choices:

1. Skip the trip.
2. Go on the trip and stop breastfeeding.

But because this device exists, I had only one choice, in my guilty-working-mother mind: Store up 300 ounces of milk in five months. Go on the trip, bring a pump and lots of batteries, and pump and dump six times a day for a week. Do this on airplanes, in the backs of moving Land Rovers, in the crowded domestic terminal of the Kathmandu airport while wrapped in a shawl (please do not attempt this), in bathrooms of all levels of hygienic upkeep, in a parked car in a field while two boys on bicycles watched me through the window, and in the presence of my company's CEO. Then come home and keep breastfeeding. This duality of freedom and burden was never more obvious to me than during that wild week.

Whether you see your breast pump as your best friend or your worst enemy, if you're going to pump at work, you need to get to know this machine. Just beware: you may become so close that you start to hear actual words in place of the pump's sounds. My friend Emily absolutely swears that her pump says "red hot panini" over and over.

Now, it's time to choose your frenemy.

What Is a Breast Pump?

Remember: when a baby nurses, she uses both compression (squeezing) and suction to get the milk out. Hand expressing uses compression. A breast pump uses suction, but you can simulate a little bit of compression by squeezing and massaging your boobs while you are pumping.

A lot of the breastfeeding books that were written years ago and are in their zillionth edition of print will be confusing to a new mother getting ready to go back to work. They have diagrams showing a woman hand-expressing milk into a little cup, which is not really practical at work. They talk about single, manual pumps vs. double, electric pumps. Please let me clear all of this up: *If you are going back to work, you need a double electric pump.*

By all means, get yourself a single hand pump to keep next to your bed for the early weeks when your baby starts to sleep longer at night and you wake up with porn star boobs, or to bring out on date night to take the pressure off. Keep this single pump in the car or at your desk once you're back at work in case you forget your pump or an essential part of it one day (this will happen).

Learn to hand express as well, but do not confuse either tool with the milking machine you will need at work. For the average woman, trying to hand express milk every day at work would be impractical, although I do know of women whose bodies don't respond to the pump and who, amazingly, successfully use hand expressing while at work. Some women use a hand pump at work, but it does take at least twice as long (because, two boobs, ladies) and might eventually give you Incredible Hulk muscles in your hands. This isn't a hard-and-fast rule, but most of us go double electric and never look back.

Choosing Your Pump

I am pretty conservative when it comes to breast pump choice. I figure best-selling must mean something, so I used the Medela Pump In Style twice. (They're not paying me to say this.)

There are other reputable brands out there—Lansinoh, Ameda, Avent, and Hygeia, for example—and I think the choice really comes down to asking your friends and your lactation professional and, since the Affordable Care Act requires nearly all health insurance plans to cover breast pumps, seeing what your insurance company provides.

If you are shopping around, pay attention to:

- Cycling rates: A cycling rate between 40 and 60 times a minute is best, as this mimics a baby's sucking. Anything under 30 is probably too slow. This information can be hard to find on some pump brands. Most of the major brands will fall within this range, but if you're curious or concerned, give their customer service line a call.
- Suction (vacuum) strength: La Leche League suggests vacuum pressure of 220 to 230 mmHg. Anything above 250 mmHg could hurt. Not every pump advertises this information on the box, so you might need to investigate.

- Open vs. closed system: A "closed system" pump has mechanisms in place to prevent moisture from getting into the tubing and machinery of the pump. An "open system" pump does not, meaning that there is a small chance that milk could get into the motor, creating a contamination risk. Open-system pumps are not considered safe to share or re-use. Most Medela pumps are "open," and while some see this as a drawback, Medela is still a popular brand. Multi-user pumps (more on this in the next bullet point) are required to be closed-system. Ameda, Elite, Lansinoh, and Hygeia offer closed-system pumps; Lansinoh, for one, has voluntarily made even its single-user pumps "closed."
- Multi-user vs. single-user: Multi-user pumps are required by the Food and Drug Administration (FDA) to be closed-system. The "multi" part means that multiple women can use them as long as each person uses her own collection kit (flanges, connectors, bottles, and tubes). These pumps are often more powerful and can therefore help you produce more milk, but they're expensive. Insurance companies might cover the rental or purchase cost, especially if there is a medical reason, such as having a premature baby. Do note that as you look for a pump, you will see and hear about "hospital-grade" pumps. The FDA doesn't actually regulate the use of the term "hospital-grade" for pumps, so there's no standard definition. Most companies mean "multi-user, closed system" when they say "hospital-grade," but you should do your research on any pumps that use that term.

- Warranty: Make sure your pump offers a warranty of a year or more. This can be a good indicator of durability. Many pumps are at their best for about a year, and motors may decrease in strength after that. If you're curious about your motor strength, have it checked out by a lactation professional or at a maternity store that sells pumps.
- Updates and new models: There are innovations happening all the time in breast pumps, to the point where I'm sure my daughter will see a photo of my pump someday and marvel at the medieval nature of the thing. Check out what the major pump manufacturers are up to.

If you buy your pump, check with your health insurer and employer first (sometimes they will cover all or part of the cost) and claim your tax break. Breast pumps qualify as a healthcare expense, meaning you can use pre-tax money from a flexible spending account.

Understanding the Pump Parts

The parts of your pump vary based on the make and model, but they boil down to a few things:

- The pump machine. This is usually housed inside a bag, with a power cord, an on/off switch, and usually one or two dials to control the suction and speed of the pump.

- The horns that go on your boobs. These are called "flanges" or "shields," and they will spend more time touching your boobs than your high school boyfriend.
- The plastic things that attach to the flanges. I actually had to look up what these are called as I was writing this book. Apparently they are the "connectors."
- For many pump models, the little white membranes that attach to the connectors. These are far more important than they look, and they have a knack for disappearing.
- Tubing. Tubes plug into the connectors on one end and into the pump on the other. They are not where the milk flows through. The pump forces air through these tubes to create suction.
- The power cord. Some pumps also offer a battery pack.

Improving on Your Pump's Basic Parts

You might be thinking, "That's all I need, right?" No, unless you plan to never leave the house. Aside from what Samantha, a news producer I interviewed, says is the essential item for pumping at work—"a really thick skin"—there is additional gear that will make your life easier.

New flanges

Standard pump flanges stick straight out from your body, so to avoid spills, you have to sit ramrod straight, then hunch forward while pulling the flanges off. I swear that I am not on the payroll of this company, but you can solve this problem by going online to Pumpin' Pal (www.pumpinpal.com) to buy a set of angled flanges. That angle makes all the difference in the world.

Another consideration with flanges is size. Women have different breast, areola, and nipple sizes, so testing sizes can help with both production and comfort. When pumping, your nipple will be drawn into the tube of the flange, and with a proper fit, your nipple should not be rubbing against the sides of that tube.

Battery pack and car adapter

If your pump offers these attachments, keep them and back-up batteries with your pump at all times. If you know you'll be in the car or other weird locations to pump, and your chosen pump brand does not offer these options, you might want to reconsider your choice. A friend gave me a plug-in battery charger and rechargeable batteries, which was a nice money-saving addition.

Also of note: It took me until I was in another country to realize that my battery pack had two sides, each holding four AA batteries. I had been replacing only the batteries on one side and wondering why the pump was so slow.

Bag

Nobody is fooled by the "briefcase" that your pump comes in. Okay, maybe men are fooled by it because they don't notice anything, but women are not. If you care, you can buy a specialty bag designed with style and functionality in mind. Nurse Purse is a good place to start because their bags are spill-proof, nice-looking, and made to hold breast pumps, laptops, and more.

Cooler bag for trucking milk back and forth

Get an opaque cooler bag and ice packs, or freezable lunch bags that can remove the stress of remembering ice packs. A lunch bag size works for a workday or a business trip of one or two days. You'll need something that would hold a six-pack of beer (and hopefully will, in the future) for a longer time away.

Your Packing List

Start by packing your bag with everything you might need and pare down over time as you learn what works for you.

Routine and preparation are your friends. One option: every night, pack the pump bag so you can grab and go in the morning. One woman I talked to had her husband do this, which took some stress off of her. He even pre-assembled all the pump parts for her. If it were me? Leaving this to my husband would have made me paranoid that he'd forget something (which, I love him, but he would).

First day at work pump bag packing list

- 1 reusable lunch bag or small cooler bag
- At least 4 milk bottles with lids
- 2 connectors with membranes intact
- 1 package of extra membranes
- 2 flanges/horns
- 2 sets of tubing
- 1 battery pack with batteries
- 1 Medela microwave sterilization bag
- 1 pack of Medela sanitizing wipes
- 1 bottle of hand sanitizer
- 4 extra breast pads
- 1 small pack of wet wipes (for spills)
- 10 breastmilk storage bags and a Sharpie to label them
- 5 gallon-size Ziploc bags with the slider to zip shut
- 1 hand pump

Chapter 3: Pumping School

Welcome to School

Now you own a ton of weird stuff you never knew you'd want or need. So let's learn how to use the &%@# pump.

Pumping makes many women feel like farm animals. For me, it is everything actual nursing is not: sanitized, cold (sometimes literally, if you've just washed the parts or tend to keep them in the fridge at work in between sessions), stressful, and industrial. It was also totally and completely foreign to me, up until the first time I tried doing it, which is where Pumping School comes in.

Unless they make you pump in the hospital (which happens for some women), you might find yourself at home, with a baby and a very porn-star-esque pair of boobs, wondering who the hell is going to show you how to use this thing.

I am a visual and tactile learner, and I needed someone who could see me with my shirt off to show me how to do it. So my best friend Karen took me to Pumping School. Her older sister had done Pumping School with her, and I have since taught Pumping School sessions with my own sister as well as several other friends. I imagine us like a bunch of cave people passing down life lessons from woman to woman—except with a weird machine on our boobs.

How to Get Taught

Between weeks three and six of your baby's life, you should invite to your home a mother with recent experience with pumping breastmilk (you don't want your pumping professor's last pumping experience to have been with a 1970s "bicycle horn" manual machine). This should be a woman with whom you are comfortable seeing both of your newly gigantic boobs.

Tell her that she is coming over to teach you how to use a breast pump. You will not beat around the bush on this. You will have waiting at your house your pump and its basic parts, breastmilk storage bags, and a Sharpie or other permanent marker.

Time this little date so your friend comes by just before the first morning feeding (or during, if she has a key or you have someone else to open the front door for her while you have a baby attached to you). If she has a toddler, find a way to suggest that she leave this lovely small person at home.

This friend will come over and, if necessary, unpack your pump from its box for the first time and clean the parts. (Perhaps you have left it in the box in a closet, unsure what the hell you'd do with it, when, and how. Believe me when I say that you are not alone. I had to unseal the tape from the box of my sister's breast pump when I arrived at her house when her son was about four weeks old.) Your friend will then be patient while your baby totally screws up the feeding schedule.

You're going to feed your baby as normal, then pump immediately after the feeding. I recognize how silly and arbitrary a term like "first morning feeding" is, given that for many of us this could be 12:17 a.m., 2:52 a.m., 5:03 a.m., or 7:30 a.m. What the books mean (and what I mean) when they say "first morning feeding" is the first one that occurs at a time that seems remotely reasonable and sustainable for a happy life, marriage, and parenting experience. Just pretend that any feeding at or after 6:00 a.m. is the first one of the day, even if it isn't and it makes you want to throw this book against the wall.

The reason you'd shoot for the first morning feeding for pumping is that your body is making more milk at this time of day. Also, if you pump immediately after a morning feeding, it can help trick your body into making a bit more milk throughout the day. However, if for some reason you just can't do this time of day, it is not the end of the world. Any time of day will work.

Once you've actually been able to nurse, your friend will set you up with the pump—placing the parts onto your boobs if need be—and have you pump for the first time. She will show you how most modern pumps have an initial "letdown" setting, which pumps quickly and with less suction, to simulate the way your baby sucks when she is first on your breast. Your friend will show you how this letdown setting then switches over to the general setting, resulting in slower and deeper suction cycles, again to simulate what your baby does once the milk starts flowing. And she'll show you the little dial that you can use to control how strongly this machine suctions your boobs.

Note: You can work your way up to the highest setting on this little dial, and you should pay attention to what setting works best for you—it isn't always the highest one. If this is your first time pumping, I wouldn't recommend trying that highest setting. You can eventually get there, but it would not be comfortable to start off there.

Break for Questions

Here's what you might worry about in this process:

1. If I pump after I feed the baby, will I have enough milk for the next feeding? Yes, you'll be fine. Your breasts are always making milk and you don't need to "fill up." In fact, you will probably produce more milk that day because of the increased demand.
2. Will there be any milk to pump since my baby just finished eating? Maybe. Maybe not. This first time around is just for practice, so don't sweat it if all you see is a few drops.
3. Am I really going to do this several times a day when I go back to work? Um, yes. If you want to breastfeed after you're back at work, you are probably going to pump at work. It's not fun, but it is doable.
4. Who is going to hold the baby while I do Pumping School? Options: your Pumping School teacher, your spouse, a baby swing or chair, or the floor.

Back to School

During the first fifteen minutes or so (which aren't going to feel awesome), you might produce just a couple of drops. Or you might produce four ounces and feel awesome and/or like a cow. There is no definition of success, other than learning how to do it and experiencing it so it stops seeming so foreign and weird. (Note: It will never completely stop seeming foreign and weird.)

You are going to see, for example, that your nipples are stretching to a greater length than you thought possible (a friend described seeing his wife pumping for the first time as "two thumbs in a garden hose"). You are going to realize with horror that this is what is happening to your nipples every time you nurse your baby.

You are going to wonder what will happen to your sex life if/when (it's a "when," trust me) your partner sees this process. It will be awkward, but you'll both survive it.

Your first time, you might be surprised to see what your breastmilk looks like. It can be thin and watery or thick and creamy. It can be white, yellowish, bluish, or greenish. In fact, it will be all of the above (which is normal) at different times of the day and over time.

Congratulations. You've just joined the most exhausted, most multi-tasking, most ass-kicking club of women in the world.

Chapter 4: Bottles and Freezer Stash

To Schedule or To Demand-Feed

If you are feeding your baby on demand, when it's time to go back to work, you have two choices: let your caregiver know that you want your baby to continue to be bottlefed on demand, or start moving your baby to a more scheduled feeding routine.

If you want to have your baby fed on demand while you're at work, you will still want to get yourself on a pumping schedule at work, since pumping with the same frequency as a demand-fed baby is not usually compatible with putting in a productive workday.

If you're the scheduling type for your baby, you will probably have an easier time making sense of how often you need to pump and how much milk you need. There are many resources available for moving your baby, gently and safely, to a feeding schedule. They range from the attachment parenting school to the parent-led school. As long as your baby is nourished and hydrated, do what works for you and your family.

Introducing the Bottle

If you're going to go back to work, you're going to have to teach this baby how to use a bottle. And even while still at home with the baby, the combination of milk stash and bottle readiness can be a great physical and mental relief. I found myself really needing to feel that I could leave the house for more than ten minutes without imagining my baby howling with hunger back at home. Plus, it's a lovely bonding opportunity for your spouse or a grandparent to get to give the baby a bottle now and then.

Bottle introduction freaks a lot of new mothers out because of the risk of "nipple confusion" (also a good name for a punk band), meaning that the baby might start to prefer bottle to breast. Working mothers also have to deal with the fear that the baby won't take a bottle at all when it's time to go back to work.

Stressful bottle situations can happen in both directions, and it's best to seek out a lactation professional if things are not working well. But with patience and good planning, most people can help their babies learn bottle skills without too much drama.

I went straight to the experts on this one, consulting lactation professionals and a friend who is both an intrepid at-work pumper and a pediatrician herself. According to them, the basics of bottle introduction are as follows:

- Start three to six weeks in. After six to eight weeks, babies lose their suck reflex and could get choosy.
- Use a small amount of milk: one to three ounces.
- Have someone other than you give the first few bottles. Some babies (not all) will never happily take a bottle from mom, and a few stubborn little guys flat-out refuse to let mom give them a bottle. But with patience, almost all babies will take a bottle

from others. You might even want to leave the room (or the house!) for the first few tries.

- Give the first bottle about halfway between normal feedings—about an hour after the previous feeding. This is to make sure the baby is not super hungry, so he doesn't really need the milk and get frustrated that it's not coming from a boob. This first bottle is practice, not a full meal.

- Make sure you have the slowest flow nipple on the bottle (called "Level NB" or "Level 1" in most major brands). You don't want him getting used to fast flow, then getting mad at your boobs for being too slow.

- Don't expect the baby to get it on the first try. Many babies require a few tries over the course of a few days or a week. Don't push it, and don't panic. When my son first rejected a bottle, I went immediately to a dark place of "I'm never going to be able to go back to work; I'm going to be tied to this baby until college; how will I afford college if I can't go back to work?" I was wrong.

- Keep the bottle in the mix, even if it's way before you go back to work, in order to keep your baby's bottle skills up. Offer a bottle at least once or twice a week. Give pumped breastmilk or formula for a bottle feeding and pump while the baby is eating. If you don't have any breastmilk and don't want to use formula, you can pump fifteen minutes before the feeding and use that milk for the baby's bottle. This will give you more practice with pumping, and give other caregivers extra bonding time.

- If you've tried and it's not working, experiment with different bottles and nipples (borrow from friends if you don't want to buy a bunch of new stuff), and consult your pediatrician and/or lactation professional.

Burning Questions

With bottle readiness underway, it's time to start working on that breastmilk stash. Once you start thinking about your first day back at work—whether it's while you're still in the hospital or the week before your leave is over—you're likely to have some questions about how to make and handle the milk you hope to leave with your baby's caregiver:

1. How do I start saving up breastmilk before I go back to work?
2. How much breastmilk do I need in the fridge/freezer before my first day back at work?
3. How do I store milk?
4. How do I know milk is safe to use?
5. How do I train caregivers on giving breastmilk?
6. What happens if my milk stash runs out?

1. How Do I Start Saving Up Milk?

Once you've learned how to pump, your next step is getting on a regular schedule of pumping and saving breastmilk.

Bottles and Freezer Stash

You know about supply and demand—that perfect cycle of your body making as much milk as your baby needs. This might make you wonder how you will ever get any milk to save for when you go back to work. I don't think it's coincidence that internet search terms like "milk stash back to work" are one of the most common ways that people find my blog.

Believe me that building a milk stash is entirely possible, assuming you have a pretty normal milk supply. If you have low supply and/or are already supplementing with formula, you will have to work harder to store up milk, and you might be looking at some supplementing during the day. And you are still an awesome mom.

There are two pretty good times of day to get that extra milk:
1. Pumping immediately after the morning (6 or 7 a.m.) feeding.
2. Once your baby is sleeping longer hours at night, pumping while she is asleep.

Let's focus on #1, since #2 is much less predictable. Most women's milk is more abundant in the morning, so pumping at this time is ideal. It also offers the benefit of setting you up for a more milk-productive day, by kicking the day off with some additional demand. Feed and burp your baby, set her up somewhere comfortable, and sit down to pump.

In the first few days or weeks you might get very little milk, but you will see the volume go up over time, and if your baby stretches out for longer and longer nighttime sleeps, you will wake up fuller in the morning and have more milk to spare. The milk you pump can go straight into a freezer bag or in a storage bottle in the fridge until you have enough to fill a freezer bag. Within a few weeks, you will have a nice little supply.

Please, please take note: you do not have to do this additional pumping every single day. Some days you will be tired. Some days your baby will need you, or you'll just plain not feel like it. Give yourself a break. It's gonna be okay.

2. How Much Milk Do I Need?

The obvious answer to this question is that you need enough milk to get your baby through a single workday of feedings. This is based on the premise that you will pump enough on your first day back at work to replenish your at-home supply. But taking into consideration the stress and emotion of the first day back, plus navigating your way to find the time and space to pump, it's best to have a bigger stash at home while you get your routine worked out. Let's call that three workdays as a goal.

If you are breastfeeding most of your baby's feedings (rather than bottle feeding formula or expressed milk), you might have no idea how many ounces of milk your baby eats during a typical day. You might think you can figure it out by doing a whole day of bottle feeding your expressed milk while you pump during or just before feedings, but this actually isn't a great idea. Because babies can very easily overfeed from a bottle, and because some women's bodies don't respond as well to the pump as to the baby, you could end up confusing yourself further.

I'd suggest going with experts' estimate of what a normal infant eats: on average, 26 ounces per day. Keep in mind that every baby is different, and this is an average, so your baby could be eating more or less than that by a few ounces—and of course, babies don't eat the same amount at every feeding. But that's okay; we're just trying to get a reasonable number to shoot for.

Divide that 26-ounce figure by the number of feedings your baby is on per day (this varies, but is probably between six and twelve feedings for a two- to four-month-old baby), and figure out how many feedings you will miss while at work. There's your magic number for a single workday.

For example, let's assume the following:

- My baby needs 26 ounces of breast milk per day
- She is doing six feedings in a 24-hour period when I go back to work
- 26 ounces divided by six feedings = a little more than 4 ounces per feeding
- In a 9-to-5 workday I will miss three of her feedings (10 a.m., 1 p.m., and 4 p.m.).
- Three feedings times a little more than 4 ounces = I need to leave her caregiver with between 12 and 14 ounces of breastmilk for a single day.

Another way to look at it: A baby needs 1 to 1.5 ounces of milk for every hour he is away from you, his source of milk. So for my 9-to-5 workday, which is eight hours, he would need between 8 and 12 ounces.

You can see that depending on how you calculate what your baby needs, you will end up with different numbers. Don't stress about this. Remember, we are just trying to get to a decent target.

I am a worrier and an over-planner, and I would stress about things like growth spurts and spilled milk, so I would probably shoot for 15 ounces for a workday. For a three-day stash, then, I would need 45 ounces of milk.

I know this figure looks daunting on paper, and you might be wondering where and when, exactly, you will get 45 ounces of milk. It is doable if you start early. Even if I were to "bank" only two ounces a day, within three weeks I'd hit my goal, and many women will get much more than a couple of ounces out of that morning pumping session as time goes on.

If you have a short maternity leave or no leave at all, don't panic. A single day's worth of breastmilk is great. And supplementing with formula is not the end of the world. Honest.

If you think or know you will have business travel in your near future, you have some additional decision making to do. Being away from your baby for one or more overnights is not only heart-wrenching, it requires quite a lot of milk in the freezer if you want your baby to get only breastmilk while you're away. Go back to that 26-ounce amount—that is the average for a 24-hour period. So a three-day business trip would use up something in the neighborhood of 78 ounces of milk. Of course, you will be pumping on the road and can try to bring that milk back with you, which will be covered in Chapter 13.

3. How Do I Store Milk at Home?

Whatever you produce, you have to figure out how to store expressed breastmilk since you'll be doing this multiple times a day at work.

I have found that Lansinoh milk storage bags leak less than Medela brand, but would still recommend always transporting bagged milk (liquid or frozen) inside another Ziploc bag and thawing frozen milk inside a bag or other clean, closable container (like a Tupperware) to catch any leaks.

As for pouring, I got all the way through my first baby, and nine months into breastfeeding my second baby, before I stumbled along this trick in an online comment to a blog post I wrote about pumping: Use the breast flange as a funnel to pour milk from bottles into bags. Genius!

There are a few ways to ensure you have milk for your baby while you're at work, and they are not mutually exclusive. You will probably end up using most of these tactics at some point.

Option 1: Day-by-day pumping

With this option, everything you pump today goes into bottles for tomorrow. The downside is that if you spill milk or have a low-production day, or your baby has a growth spurt, you might not have enough milk for the next day. This is where a freezer stash is helpful.

Option 2: Freezer stash

Using the tactics described above, you can build up a freezer stash ranging from dozens to hundreds of ounces of milk.

There are three basic schools of thought on how much milk to freeze in bags. Some women prefer to do three ounces at a time, making little pouches of milk that give them a more nuanced ability to decide how much milk to thaw.

On the other end of the spectrum is women who fill the bag almost to the top, to maximize what it can hold. I found that my comfort level on "full" worked out to about eight ounces. I have a friend who swears she fit eleven ounces into those suckers.

Somewhere in the middle is the five-ounce approach since it's close to the maximum stomach size of an older infant. Over time, you can play around with what makes you comfortable, including storing a mix of sizes so you have some larger bags and some mini-bags to thaw quickly when just a bit more is needed.

Whatever volume you choose, squeeze the air out of the bag and write the date on it with a Sharpie. Get into the practice of adding your initials if you think you'll share a fridge or freezer at work. Some women also list number of ounces. If you do this, read the ounces while the milk is still in the pump bottles; once the milk is in the bag it's hard to accurately read the volume. I gave this practice up long ago, because I just don't have the energy for it, so I have learned how to eyeball a freezer bag.

If you like detail, you also can write the time of day on the bag. Milk changes somewhat throughout the day, and some people like to give their babies milk that was pumped at a similar time of day as the feeding. This is not a must-do; it's too much for me to even think about.

Now the milk goes into the freezer. I learned to lay the bags flat on their sides, which allows them to freeze into stackable bricks. An additional trick I have seen is to freeze them flat and then store these bricks, standing upright, in a shoebox in the freezer with the oldest in front. You can pull individual bricks from the front when you need them, and add new bricks to the back once they're frozen.

To thaw, move your oldest frozen bags into the fridge and give them a full day. If you're in a rush, put the bags in a bowl of warm or hot water (never boil or microwave breastmilk, in any container). Either way, when thawing milk, remember to seal the milk bags in Ziploc bags or clean containers first to catch any milk that might leak.

Note that freezing reduces some of the beneficial properties of breastmilk, but certainly not all of them. Please don't start to worry that giving your baby frozen/thawed milk is bad for him.

Option 3: Formula

With my first child, I was obsessive about exclusively breastfeeding. People would ask me, "Are you breastfeeding?" expecting a yes/no answer, and I would reply, "YES! Not one drop of formula has crossed his lips in seven months, three weeks, and four days!" (I cringe when I remember this version of myself.)

When my daughter was born, I bought a can of formula, just in case. My husband gave her two ounces when she was six weeks old, just to test it out. It reduced my pretty significant anxiety just to know that there was a back-up option if someone spilled the breastmilk or if I had a low-production day.

You will know within a couple of hours whether your baby will tolerate regular formula (some babies have issues with the cow's milk it is derived from). If she gets fussy or gassy soon after, develops a rash or hives, starts vomiting, or has weird poop, talk to your pediatrician. You can test out different formulas and find one that works for your baby.

I should note that there is solid scientific evidence to suggest that introducing formula in the first few months can impact the good bacteria in a baby's gastrointestinal tract, creating an increased chance for allergy or illness in the baby. For some women, this is an important consideration when deciding whether to give formula. I'm not telling you this to put any pressure on you, but I wouldn't be doing my job if I didn't tell you this so you can make your own informed decisions.

Option 4: Donor milk

This can be expensive to purchase, as from a milk bank (these organizations do amazing work, and that costs money!). You could also investigate, to your comfort level, informal milk-sharing networks, such as Human Milk 4 Human Babies.

4. How Do I Know Milk Is Safe to Use?

The internet is your friend and foe on a lot of things related to parenting, and use of breastmilk is no different. Guidelines for how long you can store and use breastmilk range, a lot:

- At room temperature: 4-8 hours
- In the fridge: 72 hours to a full week
- In the freezer: 3-6 months, or a year with a deep freezer
- Frozen, then thawed: good in the fridge for 1-3 days

All of this depends on whom you ask—and also on what number kid you're on (what seemed risky for a first baby will sometimes end up feeling fine for a second or third). You will have to find your own comfort level. I really believe in the stability of breastmilk, so I lean toward the longer recommendations.

On the topic of usage: If you're going to be dealing with breastmilk in fridge and freezer form, bite the bullet and taste your milk. Take a tiny taste in newly expressed, refrigerated, and frozen/thawed form (more on what to do if your thawed milk smells or tastes "off" in Chapter 17) so you know what good milk is supposed to taste like. If you can, get your spouse to do the same (not something I ever accomplished at my house). Knowing what "normal" tastes like can help you make decisions. I rely on my nose and, if absolutely necessary, my taste buds, along with the usage guidelines, when making keep-or-toss decisions.

Along with time in the fridge or freezer, most women have questions about whether they can combine milk from different pumping sessions or re-use breastmilk from a bottle that the baby didn't finish the first time around. Combining batches is fine as long as you follow a few rules:

- Milk should be the same temperature before it's combined, so chill fresh milk before adding it to fridge milk.
- Don't combine new milk with super old milk.
- Date the combined milk according to the oldest milk used.
- You can even add liquid milk to frozen milk, as long as the liquid milk is cold, so it doesn't thaw the frozen milk.

If you're wondering if you can give your baby breastmilk left in the bottle from a previous feeding, you will find a range of answers. Some experts say that you have to discard whatever is left in the bottle after a feeding. La Leche League, however, says you can re-use milk once, and I like that option because I hate throwing away breastmilk.

5. How Do I Train Caregivers on Giving Breastmilk?

Leaving your breastmilk with a caregiver—be it your spouse, a nanny, a day care, or a relative—can be stressful. You might worry that no one will treat your precious milk with as much care as you do. You might have concerns about the caregiver handling the milk safely, and you will probably stress about how much breastmilk the caregiver gives to your baby, especially in comparison to how much you are pumping at work.

Training your family and caregivers on those usage guidelines (including keeping a large chart on your fridge and at your daycare) and on how to thaw frozen milk is an essential part of protecting your baby and your stash.

Here's what can happen when you don't train those who will be handling your milk:

> Melissa had work travel for three days. She pumped and brought back a cooler full of milk, relieved at being able to replenish her freezer stash. The next day she went to work, and her husband thawed out a frozen bag to give to the baby. The bag leaked and most of that milk was lost. So he took all fifteen bags out of the freezer (why? whyyyyy????) and thawed them in a bowl of water. Another one of those bags had a leak, which was evident from the water in the bowl becoming cloudy, so he (again: why?) threw every last bag away.

Walk family and caregivers through the storage and thawing points above. Ask them to call you before throwing any milk away. Remind them never to shake milk—this is tempting because the creamy part can separate and tends to cling to the bottle or bag. While the evidence is slim, some experts say that shaking breastmilk can damage some of its components (but it's still safe to drink, so if someone does shake your milk, don't toss it). Instead, teach them to swirl the milk, tornado-style, until the creamy fat re-joins the rest of the milk.

It's not just safe milk-handling that you have to consider: I have lost count of how many working mothers have told me that caregiver-overfeeding is at the top of the list of their breastfeeding worries. Make sure to set up an ongoing dialogue with caregivers about how much milk your baby should be getting per feeding.

The risk of overfeeding is greater with a bottle than with the breast. While the milk flow will slow down with the breast over the course of a feeding, requiring the baby to work harder for it, a bottle will continue to deliver milk at the same rate. Wiggling the nipple of a bottle in a baby's mouth can also stimulate his sucking reflex, causing him to keep sucking when he's not all that hungry anymore. And there is also that very human tendency to want to see a baby finish the bottle.

Understanding how much a baby tends to need per feeding, on average, is important. Every baby is different, so don't be rigid about these numbers—instead, use the numbers, plus your mother's instinct, advice from your pediatrician and lactation professional, and your baby's hunger cues:

- Up to a month: 2 ounces or less
- 1 month to 6 months: 2.5 to 5 ounces
- 6 months and up: decreases over time

If your baby is significantly blowing past these per-feeding volumes, work with your caregiver to see if you can reduce bottle size while keeping your baby happy, fed, and hydrated. Some tips to help keep overfeeding to a minimum:

- Try dropping 0.5–1 ounce per bottle and seeing if your baby seems happy with the feeding.
- Use slow-flow nipples (start with newborn or "1" size).
- Try a pacifier after a feeding, to see if simply sucking on something will comfort the baby.
- Google and learn about "paced bottle feeding," a technique that many lactation professionals recommend.
- Talk with your caregiver to make sure he or she understands that feeding is not a solution to every cry or sign of fussiness. If you feel that your caregiver just doesn't get (or agree with) this, start looking for a new caregiver.

6. What If My Milk Stash Gets Depleted?

Whether it's a single workday or a week-long trip away from your baby, there is always the chance that your stash of milk at home will be depleted. Spills happen (try not to murder the person who does this). Power outages happen, and they can spoil milk stashes. Babies go through growth spurts.

You need a back-up plan, because you don't want to be on the phone with your frantic caregiver while your hungry baby is screaming her face off. One option, as noted earlier, is to test out a couple of ounces of formula on your baby while you are still on maternity leave. Let your spouse give a bottle of formula while you pump (and that's a whole feeding's worth of milk that you can bank). If you have your baby sorted on formula, you have it as a back-up just in case of total disaster. Some women prefer not to give any formula to their babies, so whether you take this step or not is entirely up to you.

If you are serious about maintaining your supply, and about avoiding formula, you will need to use your freezer stash for only two purposes:

- Back-up in case of spills and other emergencies.
- Replacement stash for milk you will pump during workdays or business trips.

If you begin to see your freezer stash as a way to supplement because you are not pumping enough, you will be telling your body that its current supply is fine and that it doesn't need to make any additional milk. This will get you stuck in a supply plateau if you supplement consistently—and it will slowly but surely deplete your freezer stash. This is fine if this is what you want to do, but you just need to be aware of the ramifications as they relate to whatever your breastfeeding goals happen to be. Otherwise you'll wake up one day and your stash will be gone and you will need to start supplementing with formula—and you will blame me for not warning you about it.

The Most Important Part

What you are about to do is HARD. Having and raising a baby is hard, and adding work and pumping takes it to a new level. Be kind to yourself—as kind as you'd be to your best friend in the same situation. If you're not making enough milk to get your baby through the day, you're not a failure. Seek help, yes, but don't see formula supplementation as an enemy or a sign of defeat.

If your job is so hectic that you can't get in the pumping that you need, know that by working, you are providing for your family in an important way. If you love your job, you are also doing something that fulfills you. I believe you are allowed to still value yourself and your happiness after having children. If you throw in the towel on breastfeeding at some point, for your own reasons that are not anybody else's business, please, please remember this: *your worth as a mother is not measured in ounces.*

Chapter 5: Clothing

Your Fashion Battle Is Not Over

Good news! You no longer have to shop for maternity clothes! Thank God, because it was so difficult to find cute things.

Bad news, on a couple of fronts. First, don't put those maternity clothes away yet. You're going to need them for a few months. You're definitely walking (okay, hobbling) out of that hospital looking at least six months pregnant. And if you've had a C-section, anything with a waistband is just a bad idea for a couple of weeks.

Second, now you have to get clothes for nursing and pumping. Where maternity clothes just had to accommodate your growing body, nursing clothes have to accommodate your amazingly/terrifyingly large boobs (if not on day one, then within a week or so), a (maybe) shrinking tummy, spills of milk and many other substances, and the need for your baby (and, at work, your pump) to get access to your boobs.

This results in a shockingly limited set of designs that you are supposed to make do with for the duration of breastfeeding.

Finally, here's the really bad news. You thought maternity clothes were bad? Most nursing clothes are just terrible. Except for the very expensive variety, most do not seem to be made with looking professional and halfway decent at work in mind.

The Good News

You can make normal clothes work for both nursing and pumping. Remember this: if you can nurse a baby in it, you can pump in it.

If you have a private office with a locking door, you can wear whatever you want, as long as you're comfortable sitting in your locked office with your dress pulled up to your neck or down around your waist. But I promise you that even with a lock, you'll feel exposed, and your butt cheeks will be on your office chair, which is just weird.

Your first shopping decision point is bras. You might choose to get a pumping bra: a medieval-looking device that is basically a tube bra with two nipple holes in it. Lansinoh's Simple Wishes is a pretty good version. Wait until your milk has come in to buy this thing, or you'll end up with something too small. A pumping bra provides a solid hands-free pumping experience, but it can be time consuming to put on and take off for each session. Pumpin' Pal sells a simple hands-free "necklace" that can be put on and taken off pretty quickly. If you want to go low-budget, cut your own holes into a cloth bra or sports bra.

Some women just stick their pump flanges into their regular bra cups. Others hold the flanges to themselves while they pump, but this seems incredibly inconvenient for working (a.k.a. checking Facebook). You should experiment with this bra thing during your dress rehearsal day (see Chapter 7).

Once you are bra'd up, there are two staple "nursing clothing" designs that you need to know about and largely avoid:

- The shelf top. No idea who invented this. This is a shirt with pornographic holes or slits over the nipples, and then an extra layer of fabric just across the boob area. You're meant to lift this layer up to get your girls out when it's time to pump or nurse. This thing is fooling absolutely no one in terms of looking like a normal top.
- The fake two-layer top. This looks like a V-neck with a camisole underneath. But when you pull the V to the side, you will see a gigantic slit or a hole over your boob. Nobody believes that this is actually two tops.

There *are* some nursing brands that the women I talked with do like. These include BoobDesign (some even say you can wear their stuff after you're done breastfeeding), Glamourmom, Peekaboo, and Japanese Weekend, to name a few.

What to Shop For

There are plenty of styles that are not breastfeeding clothes per se, but that you can rig up to work for you, and probably look a hell of a lot better than most of the specialty stuff.

The trick is to look for dresses and tops that will allow you to get access to your boobs without taking the garment off or pulling it up around your neck. Some ideas to get you started:

- The crossover/overlapping V-neck. Go ahead and get used to almost every shirt you own being cut like this. Wrap dresses are a good option, too, except they make a post-baby tummy even more noticeable, so whether to do this (and whether to employ some Spanx) is your call.
- Button downs. Any top with buttons is good so that you can just unbutton and go. Don't forget the "Henley" shirt—not a true button-down, but it has a few buttons at the top that can provide boob access.
- The camisole with something else on top. You can pull the top layer up and pull the camisole down to pump. (A note: We like to tell ourselves that those nursing camisoles just look like a tank top, but they don't. There are gigantic plastic snaps just above each boob to allow you to open up one side and nurse. Everyone sees these snaps, and no one thinks this is a normal tank top.)
- Cowl-necks. Enough said.

Try to avoid scoop and V-necks. They have to be pretty deep or you'll end up stretching the hell out of them, and once they're that deep, your new-and-improved boobs will be really visible in them. So unless you work at Hooters, avoid. If you do work at Hooters, it's a win-win.

While we're on the clothes topic, we need to talk about leaking. You're going to leak at work, especially in the early months. You'll get busy, and something will make your milk let down, and then you will be part of the sisterhood of women whose co-workers have seen their breastmilk on their clothes.

Those little breast pads are important. There are washable kinds and disposable kinds; I personally go disposable, because I've heard enough negative reviews of the actual leak-proofing of the washable kind. Whatever your choice, change them regularly to avoid moisture and the dreaded thrush.

On top of actual leak guards, give some thought, especially early on when you are more likely to leak, to color, fabric, and pattern. Heather gray is not your friend: it will show leaks more than any other color. Dark colors, patterns, and textured fabrics can help mask leaks. And always, always have a back-up shirt option and a cardigan stashed in your car or at your desk.

Chapter 6: Breastfeeding Rights at Work

Before you walk through the door of your workplace on your first day back, you ought to know your legal rights—if you have any—for pumping at work. This chapter will walk you through the legal protections for working, breastfeeding women in the United States. Because I am not a legal expert, note that any analysis or suggestions, in this chapter and in this book, are not legal advice. Consulting an attorney is your best bet for fully understanding and acting to protect your rights. There, I've said it.

The U.S. System

This is not a simple topic to tackle; only a good employment lawyer can provide full analysis and advice. But I have talked with lawyers, sifted through lots of legalese, and read opinions and court cases, in an effort to present at least the basic facts about what your rights are—and are not—when you want to pump breastmilk at work.

I'd advise that you keep this legal information in your back pocket to use if you need it, instead of leading with it when approaching your employer to discuss pumping at work. If at all possible, you want this conversation to be friendly, and walking in armed with legalese does not set that tone.

Here's what's important to understand in the United States: We operate on a federal system, where federal law (passed by Congress) can set a baseline for all citizens. Individual states have to follow federal law, and can (but don't have to) implement additional laws and policies that are more generous than the federal laws. In plain English, this means that there is a federal law on the books—courtesy of the Affordable Care Act (a.k.a. Obamacare)—that provides *some* rights and protections for *some* working and breastfeeding mothers.

Many women are not protected by this law, so some individual states (definitely not all of them) have additional laws that extend workplace lactation rights to more women. Some states also have language that allows employers to be breastfeeding friendly, but doesn't require them to do anything. We will get into all of this in this chapter.

Yes, this is confusing and, frankly, stupid, and we are going to have to raise our voices if we want to see universal protections that we can count on for all breastfeeding, working mothers.

Federal Law

At the time of this edition of this book, the important federal stuff happens in Section 4207 of the ACA, which provides an amendment to Section 7 of the Fair Labor Standards Act (FLSA).

It requires *some* employers to give "reasonable break time for an employee to express breastmilk for one year after the child's birth each time such employee has need to express the milk" and to provide "a place, other than a bathroom, that is shielded from view and free from intrusion from co-workers and the public, which may be used by an employee to express breastmilk."

Some notes on this language:

- "Reasonable break time" is not currently defined; it's hoped that this guidance will be forthcoming.
- Non-bathroom space doesn't have to be permanent; it can be temporary or made available when needed.
- Employers do not have to pay for break times used to pump. However, if the employee is not "completely relieved from duty" while pumping, the time must be compensated as work time.
- If an employer does provide paid break time, employees can use that time to pump, and must be compensated as they would for any compensated break time.

This sounds great, but it comes with a huge catch, sometimes called the "white collar" exemption: this law only applies to employees covered under the FLSA—known as "non-exempt" employees in FLSA lingo. In practice, this means the law applies only to federal employees (all of them) and employees in the private sector who are paid an hourly wage. In other words, if you are paid a salary and don't work for the

U.S. government, this law and its protections most likely do not apply to you.

There is also a potential exemption from the law for employers who have fewer than fifty employees, even if their employees are covered under FLSA, but these employers would have to prove significant hardship in having to comply with the law, and this is not an easy task for an employer.

Long story short: If this law *does* apply to you, your employer must provide you with reasonable break times and a private, non-bathroom place to pump. If your employer provides paid break time, you are allowed to use your paid breaks to pump.

State Laws

Where does this leave all of the "exempt" employees—essentially most women who earn a salary rather than an hourly wage?

Unfortunately, at this time, you're left at the mercy of the laws of the state you live in.

Almost all states have some laws to protect the rights of women to breastfeed a baby in public. Fewer states (twenty-four at the time of this writing) have laws that relate in some way to lactating women in the workplace.

These range from amazing (Vermont employers must provide reasonable time and a non-bathroom, private space to express breastmilk for *three years* after the birth of a child) to totally toothless (Texas allows businesses to call themselves "mother-friendly" if they have supportive policies in place—but it doesn't *require* anything of employers).

Because these laws can and will change over time (hopefully for the better), you should always look online for the most up-to-date information to understand your rights. Here are the most straightforward and up-to-date resources I have found (see Chapter 19 for web addresses):

- United States Breastfeeding Committee is an organization committed to protecting and promoting breastfeeding in the United States. The site's "Employment" section has plain-language explanations of the federal and state laws affecting breastfeeding and work. They also regularly advocate for better legislation and ask followers to get involved by contacting their Members of Congress.
- National Conference of State Legislatures maintains an online list of state laws related to breastfeeding in public and lactation in the workplace.

Individual Employer Policies

On top of this mish-mash of laws (and lack thereof), individual employers sometimes write their own policies for breastfeeding mothers. When they do, the internal policy is often more generous than the federal or state laws in place.

Check your employee handbook (if you have one) and speak to other new mothers to find out the real scoop. You can also talk to HR (more on this in Chapter 8). If your company has a policy, lucky you! You have a clear foundation on which to build your plan for pumping at work.

It's still a good idea to familiarize yourself with the federal and state laws, though, just to be sure that your employer's policy doesn't run afoul of any existing laws.

Discrimination

Discrimination at work exists, on the basis of race, religion, age, gender identity, childbearing, childrearing, disability, sexual orientation—you name it. Some lactating women do face discrimination, in the form or small or large offenses, in the workplace.

There is no guarantee that a company bound by federal or state laws will actually comply with those laws. Some women I interviewed for this book reported being treated in ways that were questionable at best and illegal at worst.

For example, a manager might take advantage of the fact that the federal law does not specify what a "reasonable" length of time is and give a woman ten minutes total to get to the lactation room, pump, and get back to her workspace. If you are protected by federal law, a manager might play dumb—or truly be ignorant of how this works—and say that since there is no state law, the business doesn't owe you anything.

The bad news is that when women fight these battles, they tend to occur one at a time, when we are already in a vulnerable state. Many women who are discriminated against or denied the ability to pump at work don't pursue legal recourse, because they need the job and are scared to lose it, can't afford the legal fees, or simply don't have the energy. So they just suffer discrimination at work, move on and find a new job, or stop breastfeeding to make the problem go away.

Should you want to take this on, there are legal resources to help you. If you feel your legal right to pump at work is being violated, or you are being discriminated against because you are pumping, try printing out the relevant legal language and approaching someone in a position of power within your company. Don't do this antagonistically—take the tone of hoping to educate and get help. If this doesn't work, find an employment lawyer. You can also file a complaint with the U.S. Department of Labor's Wage & Hour Division.

Do what feels right for your life right now, and know that if you have to choose staying at your job over breastfeeding, you are not alone, and the choice does not change the fact that you are a great mom.

Section 2: On the Job

Now that you understand the basics and have started to prepare yourself, mentally and physically, for taking on the job of breastfeeding while working, it's time to focus on the accommodations you will need, the situations you will face, and the tactics you can use to make your life easier. This section will help you figure out how to get pumping done in real-life situations, and how to at least appear, to your boss and co-workers, to be the same great, non-exhausted, totally-have-it-together employee you were before you had your baby. You are still that person, I promise. You might just have to fake it 'til you make it back to feeling that way yourself.

Chapter 7:
What You'll Need at Work

A Typical Day

Before we launch into how to navigate the your boss, your HR department, and the awkwardness of discussing your boobs and your bodily fluids with the people who sign your paychecks, let's think about what a typical day at a generic workplace might look like.

Workplaces and schedules vary widely, and if you are anything other than a 9-to-5 desk worker, take this "typical" thing with a shaker of salt. Because I could never cover every possible work setting, I'm starting you off with the most standard scenario and assuming that you, smart working mom, can tweak it based on what you know about your own situation.

You probably won't have a totally predictable baby feeding schedule when you first go back to work, unless you have a ridiculously long maternity leave (for example, do you live in Sweden?). But you can get *yourself* into a routine because you don't need to pump at the exact same time as your baby's feedings.

Sample schedule for a 9-to-5 working mother of a 12-week-old

- 6:00 a.m.: Shower and get mostly ready.
- 6:30 a.m.: First feeding of the day.
- 7:00 a.m.: Finish getting ready, have breakfast.
- 8:00 a.m.: Leave for work.
- 9:00 a.m.: Arrive at work. (Sneak in a pumping session first thing if you know you will have a busy day.)
- 10:00–10:30 a.m.: First pumping session.
- Noon: Eat lunch at desk, while working, to show your boss you are conscientious about your pumping "break" times.
- 1:30–2:00 p.m.: Second pumping session.
- 4:00 p.m.: Third pumping session, or pump on the commute home (see Chapter 11).
- 6:30 p.m.: Dinner (a.k.a. whatever your spouse has rustled up).
- 7:00 p.m.: Evening feeding.
- 10:00 p.m.: Late evening feeding.
- Wee hours: Middle-of-the-night feeding.

Note: No one's schedule looks exactly like this. Don't let it freak you out if your day is structured differently!

If you have to go back to work really soon after having a baby, as in after a few days or a few weeks, and you want to exclusively feed that baby breastmilk, you will most likely have to pump more than three times during the workday. A very new baby is probably eating ten to twelve times a day, so if you have to go back to work this early and really want to give only breastmilk, you will have to demand milk of your body ten to twelve times a day, total.

Your supply is still establishing itself at this point, and it needs your help if this is something you really want to do. If only three of these "demand" times can be at work, you're looking at a lot of make-up nursing at home and through the night to hit that magic number of feedings. This is hard—it's a lot to fit in, and, so soon after you've had your baby, your body is really still in the thick of physical (and emotional, and hormonal) recovery mode, so be gentle with yourself.

If you can't get all of that pumping in, do what you need to do. While being a new mother is exhausting no matter how you slice it, you never want to endanger your physical or mental health by pushing yourself too far. If you are going back to work really early, take it easy on your expectations of yourself and what you can do from a breastfeeding perspective. What you're doing is really hard, and you deserve grace from those around you, and especially from yourself.

Facilities You'll Need

A primer on the basics that are essential to your ability to pump:

- Private pumping space
- Time to pump
- Somewhere cold to store milk
- Somewhere to wash or store the parts between sessions

Where to Pump

In its very basic state, pumping at work requires a small private space—big enough to fit you and your pump. Also helpful: a locking door, a place to sit (for some, this means the floor, or storage boxes), a surface to put pump and bottles on, covered windows (if needed), and an electrical outlet (keep that battery pack handy just in case). If your employer is unwilling or unable to provide you with a place to pump, you'll notice that your car fits this description.

Here's what a deluxe setup looks like: A dedicated room with no windows and a locking door. Comfortable chairs or couches, and tables. Electrical outlets spread throughout the room. A multi-user pump so you only have to bring in your tubing and pump parts. A fridge and freezer. A sink and soap and a drying rack for parts. A mirror to get yourself in decent condition when you're done. Clean-up supplies like paper towels. A community bulletin board to encourage lactating mothers at the office to connect with each other. Snacks. If this is your

What You'll Need at Work

setup, all other pumping women simultaneously hate, envy, and are happy for you.

Now, wake up! There are companies that have this benefit for working new mothers, but they are few and far between. A more common lactation room scenario is just a chair, a mini fridge, and a locking door—but even that is pretty fantastic compared to what many of the women I interviewed experienced.

If your employer does not have a true lactation room, and won't provide one (more on that later), you have to start to get creative if you want a permanent, steady option for pumping. This is a worthy goal because it is both stressful and time-consuming to have to find a new place to pump every time you need to do your business.

What pumping at work looks like in practice runs the gamut of experiences. You, in a storage closet, holding the door handle because there's no lock, using the battery pack because there's no outlet. Pumping in your parked car. Walking ten minutes each way to another building when you only have a twenty-minute break total (you do the math). Chapter 11 will cover survival tips on these and many more locations.

Your basic options for a steady pumping location, if no dedicated lactation room exists, include the following:

- A private office—yours or someone else's. Great if you can get it, but you still need to address windows, locks, and whether the office culture will make people cranky that you have the door locked.

- A conference room. Locks are important, as is scheduling. If this is your lactation room, figure out a solid back-up option in case you arrive only to find a meeting in progress.
- A storage closet. If it's any consolation, many women have gone here before you.
- Your car (or a friendly co-worker's car).
- A bathroom. Not a great place to produce food for a baby, but with planning, you can keep your milk and pump sanitary. An "ideal" (using that term loosely) bathroom setup is a single-person bathroom where you can lock the door and sit on the toilet. A worst-case scenario is a stall in a public bathroom—but it's still doable.

Time to Pump

How many times you pump per day is going to depend a bit on you, your parenting style, and your baby, as well as your baby's stage of development. If your baby is in daycare or a similar childcare situation, he is probably going to take bottles on a schedule rather than feed "on demand." You could simply figure out how many feedings the baby will take while you are at work and pump the same number of times roughly on the same schedule. You do not need to time this down to the minute—nor will you be able to in a busy work environment.

If your baby is with someone who might feed him or her on demand from the bottle, shoot for pumping every three hours or so while you are at work in your baby's first three to nine months. For women with a "normal" workday, this usually works out to three pumping sessions per workday (one of these could be accomplished in the car on the way in or on the way home).

If you continue to breastfeed your baby closer to a year or beyond, you may see him dropping additional feedings, which you could make work with just two pumping sessions at work.

If you decide at any point to supplement with a bottle of formula during the day, as my friend Courtney, a pediatrician, did with both of her kids once they were six months old, you might even drop to one pumping session per workday. Just keep an eye on your supply if you do this, as different women's supplies will respond in different ways. Milk supply will go down to match demand, but many women will still produce enough milk to nurse while with their babies.

Length of pumping session depends on your body and your work schedule. You should plan on at least fifteen minutes of actual pumping (with five minutes beforehand for setup, and five minutes after for storing milk), but some women want or need twenty or thirty minutes to pump. You'll figure more of this out in your dress rehearsal—more on that in a bit.

Cold Storage

You can refrigerate or freeze your milk during the day in bottles or bags. Play around with configurations until you find one that works for you.

Some lactation spaces have a mini-fridge just for mothers. Other offices will require you to use the shared employee fridge, so be prepared to have awkward "what's that?" conversations in the office kitchen with Tim from Accounts Payable. If there is nowhere to store your milk, you might try to fit a mini-fridge under your desk, or, failing all other options, you'll have to lug a cooler and ice packs every day.

Washing and Storing Parts

Ideally, you would have access to a sink in or very near the lactation room and somewhere clean to leave the parts out to dry, too, in private. Pump parts are so weird looking that they are sure to draw looks and questions if they're left in a communal area, and who wants people touching them?

If privacy isn't an option, and you don't want to wash the parts out in the open, you can throw them, unwashed, into a Ziploc bag and put them in the fridge (or, if it's a non-mothers-only fridge, in a Ziploc and then in an opaque bag) until the next time you need to pump. This will make for a rather refreshing (meaning: cold) experience next time you pump, but it's a huge time- and hassle-saver. Many women use this trick even when there is a sink available.

If you really like to sanitize, you can also use specialty pump part wipes or a microwaveable steam-sanitizing bag (Medela makes both) to get parts clean in between pumping sessions.

Note that wet parts, whether from milk or water, are more likely to transfer water into your pump tubing. You can dry your tubing by running the pump for a few minutes at the end of each session. Just disconnect the tubes from the bottle ends and let the pump run until the tubing appears dry. Check the tubes regularly for mildew or mold, replacing them as soon as it appears.

Dress Rehearsal

Before you go back to work, give yourself a dress rehearsal of what you expect a typical day to look like.

You will be so much less stressed if you've done the whole routine once through, and know you are capable of doing it. It will help you figure out what you don't have figured out yet, like what bag you need to transport your milk across the office, how to pump in work clothes without ruining them, and how to fit everything in your pump bag and carry it across a crowded room.

Your dress rehearsal should consist of preparation, a dry run, and a wrap-up.

Preparation

It would help to have someone to help with the baby while you do this. Your baby will need to be given bottles in order for you to practice. Failing an extra pair of hands, you'll just have to muscle through it on your own.

Have one or two feedings' worth of milk ready, so you have a buffer while you practice. (See Chapter 4 for help estimating quantities.)

Dress in work clothes for the day and set up a space that is as much like what you will have at work as possible—simulate room size, whether or not the door locks, and furniture. Pack your pump bag with the gear listed in Chapter 2. Bring in your laptop and/or phone—whatever you think you'll have with you once you're back at work.

Dry run

Pump without your baby in the room, so you can work on achieving letdown on your own (photos and videos of your baby can help).

Do whatever you'll have to do at work: hold the door handle if the door doesn't lock, share desk space with a laptop, or work on emails. The point is to put yourself through the real situation before you are actually there.

After each session, pour the milk into bottles or bags. Practice packing everything up and walking across the house to your sink and fridge. This will help you realize what you need to do in your pumping space (to your milk, your pump and parts, and your own appearance) before you emerge from privacy. Get the milk bottles or bags into the fridge. Look at what you have the milk stored in and ask yourself if you're comfortable with others seeing it.

At the sink, if you plan on washing your parts rather than using the Ziploc-in-fridge trick, give them a wash, shake them to get the water out, and put them in whatever you'll use to take back to your desk. See how comfortable you will be when you have to do that at work. If the answer is "not at all," go back to the Ziploc-inside-opaque-bag idea, or get multiple sets of parts and wash them at home.

If you expect to pump in the car, go do it. Pump in the garage, in the driveway, or driving around your neighborhood. As much as this sucks (literally?), do it. It will take so much of the mystery out of the process.

Wrap-up

Do something that makes you happy. Wine? Yoga? Reality television? You've earned it.

Chapter 8:
Making a Plan
Your Boss Will Like

Talking to Your Boss about Your Breasts

Breastfeeding and working is no longer an exception for new mothers. It is no longer a valiant few women, secretly locked in closets with breast pumps; it's the new reality of an America where many women are all at once breadwinners and, for the first few months to few years of a baby's life, milk-makers.

American workplaces need to catch up to this reality. They need elements both hard (rules, policies, and infrastructure) and soft (company culture, protected by HR and executives) to ensure that every working mother has the tools to make this situation work.

Welcome to the reality of modern, working motherhood. But while we advocate and push for the world to catch up, we need solutions *now*, even if those solutions don't quite get us to the holy grail of universal support for working and breastfeeding.

Today, even in companies with lactation policies, many women are at the mercy of their particular manager or HR team. Support can make all the difference to a return to work that empowers a woman to continue to feed her baby breastmilk. Cultural and physical hurdles often mean a premature end to breastfeeding—which has implications on not just a baby's health, but a mother's attitudes toward her employer.

Like it or not, your boss is going to be your greatest ally or your biggest hurdle in your quest to breastfeed after you return to work, so it's time to figure out how to talk to him or her about your breasts.

Every Workplace is Different

I've been amazed at how widely varied the work-supportiveness thing is for the hundreds of women I've interviewed. About half of the women I heard from felt "somewhat supported" with the basics, and about a quarter of women felt incredibly well-supported, with another quarter saying they did not feel supported at all and had to figure out a lot on their own. Given the variation here, it's in your best interest to understand what managers and HR professionals expect, and what does (and does not) define success for you.

Throughout this process, the message you want to send is that when the time comes, you will be a productive member of the team. Breastfeeding your baby is fleeting, and while it's important to you, so is continuing to provide for your family and having a fulfilling work life. That means you have to stay in the game.

Even if you mean not a word of it, communicate your excitement at the prospect of leaving your perfect, tiny baby to schlep back to work. This attitude will serve you, and it also adds another proof point that women can successfully work and breastfeed, and that employers should support that.

Help Them Help You

The top thing I heard from managers and HR people is that they want to see women propose a plan for pumping, preferably before the baby is born. (If you've already had your baby, don't panic. Getting started now will get you to a good place.) They want to see an employee who has done her best to figure out what she'll need and how to make it work with her job. They want that employee to approach them in a straightforward and unentitled manner.

After talking with working mothers and a group of very helpful managers and HR people, I've got a ten-step plan for you. But before you launch into planning, you have some homework to do.

Read Chapter 6 so you know the basics of your rights. I don't suggest charging into HR waving a copy of the breastfeeding laws as a first step to building a supportive workplace environment. You need to know your rights, should it ever come to that, but remember that you want support, not antagonism. If you get to the point where you feel you need to bring up these laws, do so in an email, even if you first discuss them over the phone. You want a paper trail, just in case. But consider the "IT'S MY LEGAL RIGHT!" argument your last resort.

Make allies at work. Seek out other new-ish mothers and get them to give you the lay of the land, from where they pumped to how supportive the company was. Other candidates include the office manager or assistant who is great at solving problems, new dads (they've probably washed their share of pump parts), and grandma types who miss their grandchildren.

You will be amazed at the power of saying, "When I come back, I am going to be figuring out how to work and pump milk for my baby. If I get really stuck I'd just like to know there are a few people I can reach out to for help without it being weird." Go reach out to some people, even if you're home on maternity leave and have to do it by email. You'll feel better that you did.

Ten Steps to a Workable Plan

Here's your roadmap to a pumping plan, in short:
1. Diagnose the players
2. Write the plan
3. Approach the gatekeepers
4. Problem-solve
5. Confirm your setup
6. Go rogue (in case of roadblocks)
7. Go the extra mile
8. Check back in
9. Educate your co-workers
10. Be a good citizen

1. Diagnose the Players

Knowing that every situation is unique, you first need to figure out your best route in. In many companies, the HR department might appear to be the best place to start because they're tasked with compliance with laws and with supporting employees. But consider what this approach will say to your boss.

Debra, an HR executive, advocates that you talk to your boss first. She says, "If you go to your boss first, you're going to be a step ahead. When the employee goes to someone else, the manager starts thinking, 'Why didn't you come to me? Did you think I wouldn't support it? Are you trying to go over my head to force me to support it?'"

On the other hand, you might already know for certain that your boss does not want to have this conversation. Let's say you report to the CEO, and you know from experience that this person always prefers that you go straight to HR with anything you need on that front. You're the expert on your own situation, so do what your experience and intuition tell you to do.

The boss dynamic is often the most anxiety-inducing. How the hell do you still come across as a professional, driven woman when you have to say the word "pumping" to the person who writes your annual performance review?

One answer is: you fake it. Head high, mama. Be amazed at what you are accomplishing and proud that you are both doing your job AND keeping a whole human being nourished. Your boss can't claim that dual victory, unless she is or was a pumping mom herself. If you don't feel confident, just pretend you do until the genuine article kicks in.

When it comes to your boss, ask these diagnostic questions:

- Does your boss have children? Are they relatively young, or old enough that he or she may have forgotten what the early years were like?
- Has this person ever had someone who was pumping reporting to him or her? If so, go talk to that person, now.
- Is your boss a man? This will probably add to your anxiety, but it can also be your friend. If he finds the subject even more awkward than you do, maybe you don't ever have to bring it up again. You may find that the two of you develop a kind of code language. "I have to step out," you say. "Uh, yes, of course . . ." your boss stammers. He does not want to have this conversation. He just wants you to leave so he doesn't have to talk about it. Awesome: that's what you want, too.
- Is your boss obsessed with productivity and face time? If so, your plan will have to be well researched and airtight.

Lori, another HR exec, says you should also diagnose the culture of your organization. A progressive, liberal firm with a lot of young workers might lend itself to one type of conversation, while in a more conservative organization or one with an older workforce, you might do well to assume that people will require tactful education.

HR, if it exists, also requires diagnosis, in case you need their help at any time. Talk to other new mothers, if possible, to get their take on HR's level of support for pumping, and to find out whether there are specific people within HR to focus on or avoid.

Ask these mothers how legal-oriented HR is: do they do the bare minimum because the law requires it, or do they go the extra mile because they are awesome or because they simply want to stay on the right side of any laws? Ask if there are any differences between what HR says ("we are family-friendly") and what HR does (for example, asking a new mother repeatedly when she's going to be done breastfeeding so they can have the room back).

2. Write the Plan

Now you're going to draft your pumping plan. First, mentally look around your office environment to get a sense of where you might end up pumping. Seek out and talk to managers who have managed a breastfeeding woman. Talk to those mom-friends you made and ask them where they pumped. Ask all of these people for their advice in writing your plan.

Now think about what characteristics your plan should have. Our HR experts say a plan works best when it follows these guidelines:

- You bring it up as early as possible.
- You take a problem-solving, step-by-step approach. One executive notes, "If you say, 'When I come back to work, I want

to support my baby in this way, can you help me?' I will say, 'Well, what do you need? I don't know; *you* have to tell *me.*'" Even if the solutions are not perfect, people appreciate you putting in the effort ahead of time.

- You are specific. If you leave things undefined, people can start to think that you're taking advantage. Be up front with your boss, and with yourself, about what you will need.

- You set and manage expectations of how it's going to affect your workday. Your manager doesn't need to know the details, but she needs to know that you'll need to be gone a couple of times, for X minutes, and that sometimes it will be on short notice.

- You are clear that you're just learning how to do this. While you are on leave, learn how long pumping tends to take you (via the dress rehearsal in Chapter 7), and proactively make updates to your plan and to your manager: "Now that I'm learning, I've realized it will take a little longer than 15 minutes—it seems to be taking me 25 minutes. This will affect the plan in the following ways: _____."

- You include education. Another HR director notes, "If people haven't experienced this, you have to suck it up and educate them, no matter how awkward."

- You include a commitment to remaining productive. Lots of people don't realize that you could join a conference call or work on email while pumping. While not all managers will expect you to work while pumping, if you work in a fast-paced or time-sensitive environment, you'll gain a lot of points for offering.

- You have zero attitude of entitlement. If you want to be opinionated with your friends and spouse, do it. You don't have to set those values aside when going to work, but the attitude should be one of cooperation, not "I am owed this."
- You are honest and realistic about the structure of your day. Restrictive jobs, like answering phones in a call center, or a role that is customer-facing and requires you to be on your feet a lot, require the most planning to put your manager at ease. Are you going to be able to pump in two 15-minute breaks a day, if that's what the "normal" employee gets as break time? Maybe not. Come prepared with a plan that recognizes that you might need accommodations from your employer and proves you can make it work. Maybe this means you clock out when pumping, work longer hours, or catch up on emails while pumping. Maybe it just means that you call it out, so no one feels like you're hiding the fact that you'll be taking longer-than-usual breaks.
- You are realistic about what your company can do. "We need a chair in there" is doable. "Turn the office's only conference room into a permanent lactation room"? Not so much. Work with them on it. You are not "owed" a deluxe lactation suite, and when your breastfeeding time is over, you don't want to have burned bridges.

Now that you know what your plan should convey, write it up. Your plan should cover:

1. Where: The space you want to use, and how to make it work. Sample language:

   (If your office has a lactation room) *I understand that new mothers use _____ as a lactation room. I plan to use this space, too. What are my steps to ensure I have access to this space?*

   (If there is no lactation room) *After thinking about the office plan, I propose that I use _____ to pump.*

2. When: How often and for how long you will use that space. Sample language:

   I will need to pump three times per day, for about twenty minutes each time. I do not yet know how long I plan to breastfeed, but the American Academy of Pediatricians recommends one year.

3. What: What you need to make this work, based on input from your allies. Solve as many problems as possible ahead of time, so you are proposing solutions. If the room needs a lock on it, go talk to the office manager, then note in your plan that you have already found a potential solution.

Sample language:

The room does not lock. In order to prevent awkward encounters with co-workers, I'd like to get a lock on this door. I've spoken to the office manager, who estimates the job will cost $____ and take ____ days to complete. She is waiting for your sign-off to get started.

4. Productivity: Include points on how you will remain productive: bringing your phone or laptop with you, getting someone to cover for you, or putting in extra time at home.

   Sample language:

   I plan to block out pumping times on my calendar. Should these times conflict with an essential meeting, I will plan ahead to dial in by phone. I will work with the team to ensure this goes smoothly.

For your sake, I'd also shoot for starting back at work mid-week, if that's possible. It's helpful not to have to start with a full work week you while you make the adjustment.

3. Approach the Gatekeepers

Now that you understand the basics of what you will need, have diagnosed the people you will have to discuss this with, and have written up a draft plan, it's time to talk about your boobs with the people who pay your bills.

Every employer is different, and even within the same company, your HR point person and your particular manager will have huge influence on how awkward the conversations are and how supported you feel to get this done. Talking to people in positions of power to make pumping at work possible is awkward and often difficult. It's just a weird thing to do. None of us enjoys saying the words "pump" and "breastfeed" to a boss or co-worker. But having the conversation is the only way to get this done.

Every single HR professional I talked to recommended having this conversation before your maternity leave. With a solid few weeks to go before the baby shows up, schedule a short meeting with your boss. Keep in mind some basic ground rules for this conversation:

- Be prepared for a whole range of responses. Whatever you do, do not lose your cool. No threatening. No legalese. And no crying.

- Unless you know for sure otherwise, assume your manager is clueless about lactation. (Did you know anything about it, until now?) This doesn't mean you have to go into detail on how your breasts work, but don't assume this person is familiar with what you're going to need.

- If your boss likes this sort of thing, dig up stats about how breastfeeding can decrease illness in babies, thereby reducing your missed time from work (see Chapter 19 for resources). If your boss is really nitpicky, ask your pediatrician for a note. If your boss is neither, don't bother, as it can come across as antagonistic.

- You might already feel indebted to the company for getting maternity leave (assuming you got one), so maybe you feel sheepish asking for anything else. Do not apologize. Say thank you, but do not apologize. Practice what you will say, and practice *not* saying "I'm sorry." While you don't want to come across as entitled, you might end up regretting setting the tone that you are being done a huge favor.

Take an enormous breath and just be frank about how awkward this conversation is. Try this: "Look, this is an awkward topic and I'm uncomfortable bringing this up, but we have to have this conversation. When I come back from leave I plan to continue breastfeeding my baby, and I will need to pump milk during the workday. *(Note: you can say "express" if "pump" makes you feel weird, but a lot of people are not going to know what that means, so you might end up even more embarrassed as you have to start defining terms.)* I have drafted a plan that I think will work for everyone involved, and I want to share it with you for your input."

Some managers will instantly say, "Go talk to HR." If this happens, fine. You at least have given your boss the courtesy. You can also offer it up yourself to give your boss an easy out: "I'm happy to go to HR to figure this out, but you are my manager and I wanted to go to you first."

Don't start off scared. The horror stories are the most interesting to tell, and it seems like everyone has one. But many managers are fantastic supporters of pumping employees.

Melissa, an executive at an ad agency, knew that her office needed a lactation room once one of her direct reports got pregnant. She worked with HR to create a great space. A vaguely-worded email was sent from HR (so as not to embarrass the new mother), letting other employees know that the client lounge would be in use and couldn't be booked for the foreseeable future. The new mother was given a mini-fridge to put under her desk. Over time, Melissa and her employee developed a kind of code language for "I really need to go pump now," and Melissa worked hard to have her employee's back when she had urgent pumping needs.

If you're a total chicken, and I'm not judging you if you are, you can kick this process off by email instead of in person. Here's a sample:

Subject: Planning for my return after maternity leave

Dear _____:

I want to proactively plan for a successful and productive return to work after my maternity leave. Part of that is planning ahead for pumping breastmilk once I am back at work. This will require me to use a private room a few times every workday.

In an effort to make this process as simple and efficient as possible, I've done my homework and put together a plan that I think will work really well, with minimal impact on facilities, people, and productivity. I'd like to quickly walk you through this plan for your input, so we can get on the same page before my leave. Can we schedule time to discuss?

Thanks!

If you end up going to HR because your manager would prefer it that way, you can have a pretty different kind of conversation. This is HR's job: having awkward conversations, and supporting employees. You can tweak this conversation with HR to match your personality and the tone you pick up on from the HR person you're talking to.

Kathy, an HR exec, encourages "straight talk" to your HR rep. Practice on a friend or sympathetic co-worker. Figure out what phrasings freak you out the least.

Lori, another HR leader, suggests that you start by asking about precedent: Has this happened before? How has it been handled? If you think the mood is right, cheerfully play a little dumb: "I don't really know how this works. I have put together a plan as a starting point, but I would love your input on how this can work when I get back."

Nearly all of the HR people I interviewed suggested that being helpful, well, helps. If HR does not have a simple document explaining to new mothers how the lactation room works, draft one so it's even easier for the next new mother (and it will make HR look good). If there is a room that needs some tweaking to make it serviceable as a lactation room, offer to draft up what will need to be done. When you help them, it helps you, and it helps the moms who come next.

4. Problem-Solve

Once you have the conversation, you have a wide range of potential outcomes. You could be bowled over by the support and love you feel. You could get the feeling that as long as you don't bother this person with this, you are free to make it work on your own (not always a bad thing). You could get the distinct impression that while they technically have to let you do this (if you're protected by law or by company policy), no one is too happy about it. Or, if you don't have any legal protections, you could get a flat-out "you can't do this." You can't predict the outcomes, but you can be prepared.

If you want to address lack of support head on, put together your next round of ammunition—statistics on the business case for breastfeeding (see Chapter 19 for resources), an even more detailed plan showing how you will make it work with minimal disruption, and ideas from other women who made it work for them. Give it a few days and go back again, cheerfully. If you still hit a brick wall, maybe it's time to pull out those legal rights, if you have any—but still, cheerfully. Do everything within reason to avoid making enemies.

> Debra, an HR executive who has been on both sides of the lactation planning table, counsels, "You might get an attitude of 'if you come back, I want you back 100%.' But if you're great, wouldn't they rather have 90% of you for a year, so they can keep 100% of you for the long term? You might not say this out loud, but I'd bet the answer is yes. Know your value so you have the confidence to make your case."

Official advice aside, our working mothers have been through the ringer, and are here to share their war stories and solutions. Not all of them have perfect endings, because this is really difficult territory:

> Emily, a doctor, fought multiple battles: "Hospital staff were only allowed to use the lactation rooms if no patient needed them. So for the first month, I pumped in a bathroom. After spilling milk that was balanced on a railing, I emailed my boss

and the director of HR, demanding better conditions. They gave me a room, but it had a window. I was able to get equal access to the lactation rooms (I cited Obamacare, and had fellow moms sign a petition). But we were only allowed 15 minutes to leave the unit, gather supplies, take an elevator up, wait for a turn, pump, clean up, put supplies away, and return to the unit for work."

Kelly, a city employee, won her fight: "There wasn't a city-wide policy to support nursing moms, and my HR person was clueless and uncomfortable with the idea of me pumping. I had to fight for a designated room to pump—she asked me to schedule conference rooms, which were sometimes booked or didn't lock and someone would walk in on me. I finally told her I was going to put up a curtain and pump in my cube unless there was a dedicated room. And I got it."

Sarah, a communications professional, couldn't get past some significant barriers: "I was told to use the bathroom. Our state specifies that the pumping area cannot be a bathroom, so I educated them about state law. They found a place that met state requirements but it was long walk from my work station. I tried using offices in my building and putting up a curtain in our storage area. Eventually, I gave up pumping."

Molly, an attorney, chose to educate: "Many of the women I work with stop breastfeeding before they return to work, so the firm doesn't really get it. I had to explain to my boss that my decision to breastfeed my daughter was a medical decision, not a lifestyle decision."

Hitting a brick wall with your employer is heart-wrenching, and I don't have any easy solutions for you. Being a breadwinner for your family complicates breastfeeding, and there are a lot of factors outside of your control once you go back to work. My wish for you is that no matter what the outcome, you are able to be proud of yourself for giving it a shot.

5. Confirm Your Arrangement

When you have a plan agreed on, email HR and your boss and thank them for their support. Include whomever feels appropriate based on the conversations you've had. Ask them to reply with any notes so you are all on the same page. This also gives you their support in writing. Open and close with statements about your intention to have a productive and engaged return to work.

While you are on leave, send a reminder going over the plan:
- Remind them of your back-to-work date.
- Restate your basic needs as written up in your plan.

- Include anyone you need help from to remind them what's been agreed, and ask them to confirm that it's done.

Sample confirmation email while on leave

Hello from maternity leave! Thank you for helping me plan for this time. It's been really valuable to my family.

My return to work is scheduled for (date). I am committed to making a smooth transition, which includes the plan, re-attached here, we made for pumping. I need your help to make sure the basics are in place before I return:

(examples)

1. Lock on door of lactation room

2. Mini-fridge in lactation room

Who should I work with to confirm that these items are ready and to get a copy of the key for my first day back?

Thank you again!

6. Go Rogue

If, despite your efforts to solve problems, your boss or HR are total jerks, do not lose your cool. Hear what they have to say, thank them for their time, then go take a breather. Resistance does happen. And, unfortunately, it might happen more often to women lower in the ranks—and your financial realities might make it more difficult to say forget it, I'm just going to quit and work somewhere else. If heading out for a friendlier employment environment is not an option, you have a few ways you can just go rogue and figure this out on your own. After all, we're working mothers. We know how to figure stuff out.

If time is the problem, use whatever time you do have built into your schedule. Use breaks or a lunch hour. Use time in the bathroom, even if it's with a hand pump. Even pumping once in a workday keeps some level of supply up and provides your baby with some great breastmilk. You might have to supplement with formula, but a little breastmilk every day is a great accomplishment.

If location is an issue, step away and consider whether you need to work directly through official channels to get what you need. Figure out where you'll pump—even if it's your car, or a friendly co-worker's office, or a storage closet everyone seems to have forgotten about—and make your own space.

When going rogue, your allies will be essential. Talk to those around you about your situation, ask them to give you a little grace and coverage when you need it, and come up with code words to make it clear to them when you need to go pump.

> Jamie recounted, "The company culture was terrible, but other moms were supportive, even if it was nothing other than sharing war stories. Some let me pump in their offices."

Don't forget about your company's facilities department, office manager, or that guy who wears a tool belt and seems to make the place run. In some cases, you might bypass the system and get this guy to give you the keys to the kingdom.

7. Go the Extra Mile

If your HR team has shown desire to make the workplace great for employees, you could even suggest how they can make a lactation space really work for the new mothers on the job—or make some improvements yourself on your own time and your own dime. Being the great, amazing, helpful one in the eyes of HR can never hurt.

The following is a letter a friend of mine sent to her HR department. She works in a male-dominated industry, in a male-dominated firm, and realized that if she didn't walk HR through the process, no one would.

Super Helpful Sample Letter to HR

Dear _____,

I wanted to share ideas for enhancing the "mothers' lounge" at the office. I have focused on low-cost items that would be supportive and can enhance productivity.

- *At least two comfortable chairs.*

- *Table to set the pump and bottles on.*
- *Mini-fridge, so women can store milk without having awkward interactions in the office kitchen.*
- *Bottled water in the mini-fridge.*
- *Paper towel dispenser.*
- *Bowl of granola bars.*
- *Mirror to help get re-arranged after pumping.*
- *Whiteboard for mothers to communicate. Mutual support can even help with retention!*
- *Microwave oven, for steam-sanitizing pump parts.*
- *Suggestion box to get feedback over time.*
- *A "new moms' guide" covering policies and support measures. I would be happy to help write this.*

I am happy to discuss, and thanks for listening!

8. Check In

Once your plan is up and running, don't put it on autopilot. Elsa, an HR executive, notes that too many women forget to stay in touch with their managers on maternity leave and after.

While you're on leave, it's natural for your boss to wonder if the pull of that tiny baby will just prove too strong for you to come back to your job, so if you definitely plan to come back on the schedule you set before you had the baby, just drop your boss a line and confirm that.

You'll remove one question mark from his or her to-do list, and it never hurts to be seen as being proactive and helpful to the boss.

Once you're back at work and pumping, the checking in doesn't end. You might be tempted to never discuss pumping again with your boss, especially if the initial conversation was awkward. Don't give in to this temptation.

A few weeks into being back, give your boss an update. If everything is following your pumping plan, just say that, and say thank you for the support. This will give him or her peace that things are going according to plan.

If anything has changed that he or she needs to know about (for example, if pumping is taking you 25 minutes instead of 15), include that, and note any adjustments you are making to make it work. This keeps your manager calm, knowing that you are on top of the situation. And if he has already noticed that you are gone longer than you originally discussed, this stops him from thinking that you're taking advantage of the situation or abusing the time allotted. These things might seem unnecessary to you, but they help you look like a pro in the eyes of your boss.

9. Educate Your Co-Workers

Elsa in HR says that "co-workers are often the most forgotten group in this whole thing. You can spend so much time on your plan, and on working things out with your boss, that you forget to educate your co-workers, or those who report to you, on what's about to happen. Your co-workers and direct reports are often the ones with the least information, and they can end up feeling awkward and in the dark." And in some industries, your co-workers need to know where you are, due to safety issues, or because you're on call.

Once educated, some co-workers will get your back when you need it. Once they know what's going on, they are less likely to ask loud, potentially embarrassing questions like, "What's in the bag?" or "Where do you keep *going* every few hours?"

Handle co-worker education once, up front, in a team meeting or in one-on-ones, if that feels more appropriate. You don't have to broadcast to the whole company—just those with whom you interact regularly.

Briefly explain what you will be doing and how frequently. Acknowledge that it's an uncomfortable topic. Explain that you don't need anything specific from people, but you would appreciate their support. Then be done with it. Do not overdo it, and do not go on and on about it. Nobody you work with needs to spend half an hour talking about your boobs.

10. Be a Good Citizen

By pumping at work, you are, like it or not, a role model, a precedent, and a symbol to your co-workers of what a pumping employee looks like. You have responsibilities: to your career after you are done having babies, to the women who are pumping at the same time as you, and to the women who come after you.

First, you: You have to keep looking like a pro. Even the most supportive managers, leaders, and even some co-workers will be watching you when you come back. I heard this from several HR experts. They'll be looking at you, wondering, "Is she really the same as before? Is she as committed, and is she really back?"

Like it or not, for those looking for confirmation that you're *not* "back," everything you do at work related to your new baby can add up: every early departure for a sick kid, every time you leave a meeting to pump, every time you pull out the baby pictures to ooh and ahh with your work friends. This doesn't mean you can't do these things—our HR experts stress this point—it just means you should keep an eye on these activities and prioritize what's most essential (like pumping).

Don't let non-essential things (like too much baby talk and photo-showing) take up a lot of time or be highly visible. All that "baby stuff" gets put in the same bucket by some people, and if they get resentful that you are too focused on your baby, it could spill over into begrudging you your pumping time.

Spending too much work time on baby stuff is not a label you want to get stuck with. In the words of one sage HR pro: "Don't let other people write chapters for you—you be the author. You pen what needs to be said about you. Otherwise people will put that out there for you, and you might not like what it is."

Don't assume that you should get your pump times, plus an hour lunch, plus additional breaks. Plan to make some trade-offs and accommodations on other break times because you are adding break time by pumping. Yes, I know that it doesn't feel like a "break" to be making food for your baby. But from your employer's perspective, it's time away from your job regardless of what you're doing with it.

Worst-case scenario? *You* think: "You said I could have this time to pump." Your *manager* thinks: "She's doing a lot of socializing. I guess she doesn't appreciate the support we're giving her to pump."

Keep an eye on this relationship and on how you are spending your time. Long after your baby is weaned, you want to look and feel like someone the company can't live without.

Second, for those pumping at the same time as you: be very respectful of the lactation room. Keep it clean. It's hard for some women to let down their milk if they're not comfortable. Plus, you don't want to make management regret giving you the space. Be appreciative, and management and HR will appreciate you.

Finally, for those who come after you: don't feel overly rushed, but never abuse your pumping time. You don't want anyone to begin to suspect that you are taking more time than you need. There are always people who abuse break time, whether it's a smoke break or chatting with co-workers. Don't be that person, because it will make the road harder for the moms after you.

Chapter 9: Time, Privacy, and Awkward Co-Workers

Congratulations: You have your pump in its supposedly stylish black carrying bag that you would not be caught dead carrying if it were a regular purse. You know how to pump. You've bitten the bullet and talked to your boss, and you know where you're going to pump. Now it's time to actually start doing it, and to protect your space and time, while taking on the awkwardness that inevitably comes from mixing boobs and business.

Making and Protecting Time

All of breastfeeding and working can be hard. But what I've heard from countless women is that finding and protecting the time to pump is one of the hardest parts of the whole thing.

First of all, you're just back from maternity leave, and likely eager to prove that you are still able to do your job. Secondly, you have a backlog of work to catch up on and other people's schedules to accommodate for meetings, conference calls, and deadlines. These people are literally never thinking about your pumping schedule. With all of this, it's hard to make time for your body and your baby multiple times a day, every day.

Alisha, an account manager, blocked time off on her calendar to pump. Her boss couldn't figure out why, every day at the same times, she was blocked off and he couldn't schedule meetings. When she explained those were her pumping times, "He got really nervous. He was supportive, but I could tell it made him uncomfortable. It was actually pretty funny to watch."

Speaking frankly, some jobs are easier than others when it comes to scheduling pumping time. Some women are stuck on the floor of the Senate during a long debate, watching their own cleavage get bigger and bigger as the minutes and hours pass. Doctors in practices and hospitals may have little or no down time. Patrolling police officers and journalists can be out on the street all day. Lawyers have long days in court. Waitresses and chefs are in constant demand. Teachers have back-to-back classes with kids who are the last people they want to discuss pumping breastmilk with.

Lisa noted that, as a teacher, "One barely has time to pee, never mind pump! I was told I could use the nurse's office, which just felt too germy. I ended up pumping in my classroom, dealing with janitors and children barging in, even when the door was locked. I didn't have coverage, so I had to pump around my teaching and meeting periods."

There are simply some careers that make pumping at work more difficult. But even the more sedentary office worker can have challenges with scheduling pumping time, so our working mother experts are here to offer their best advice:

- Don't give up. Not in the "you're never allowed to quit breastfeeding" sense—only in the "tough it out for a few weeks and you're likely to figure out your own routine" kind of way. The early weeks and months are often the hardest and can seem never-ending. In breastfeeding, as in life, it's good policy to avoid making major decisions on the hardest day.
- Tell yourself again and again: doing this is your right. You are smart enough to do this *and* be valuable to the company.
- Try not to apologize—this can be difficult, but saying "sorry" suggests that you're doing something wrong.
- Ask for, and take, what you need. I heard this over and over from women who learned to do this the hard way. Don't ask in the "um, do you think that maybe, if it's not too much trouble . . ." kind of way. Ask in the "I'm going to need twenty minutes, three times a day" way. In the words of one mom, "set your boundaries early and often." It is a pretty female trait to not want to ask for what we want. Women can tend to be more reluctant to grab what's theirs, whether it's a raise or promotion, the upper hand in a meeting, or time to pump.
- Try to think of pumping as being in the same category as having to pee: It's a liquid that needs to come out of your body, and it

doesn't make sense that anyone would want to stop that from happening. Let this thought give you courage.

- Call it what it is. Many women I talked to expressed regret that they didn't just say, out loud, what they needed to do. Everyone was dancing around the word "pumping," which left them feeling awkward and embarrassed—the very feelings they were trying to avoid by not calling it what it is. Me? If someone is not getting the hint and keeps asking where I'm going, sometimes I will just say, "I have to go be a mom for a few minutes." If I'm feeling salty, I'll hit them with, "I am going to go use a machine to extract milk from my body." The stunned silence is worth it every time, and I laugh all the way to the lactation room.

- Remember that a lot of people have no idea what's happening. Breastfeeding was not widely promoted in the couple generations before us, and most people know nothing about the supply-and-demand thing, so it might not occur to people that you need to go pump. Providing milk for your baby might feel all-consuming to you, but it is not on the radar of many of your co-workers.

- Use your calendar. Block out your pumping times—call these appointments "pumping" if you're so inclined, or put them in as meetings or phone calls or private appointments. Or book them as "email" time and use a hands-free pumping bra so you can actually spend time on your inbox or similar tasks. Call it whatever makes you comfortable and makes those around you

- least likely to try to infringe upon your time. Push back when people try to double-book you.
- Pump ahead of schedule to create time for yourself when you need it. Let's say it's only 9 a.m. and you usually pump at ten, but you've got a hellish middle of the day. Go pump. Buy yourself an extra hour later.
- Use your phone. Figure out when you can call into a meeting rather than being there in person. Invest in a shawl that you can throw over your pump to diminish the sound, and use the mute button liberally while dialed in.
- Make your car your friend. Some women find commute-pumping to be one of the most relaxing ways to fit in a session. You're alone (unless you count fellow drivers on the road), the time is your own, you have music to listen to, and your focus is on something other than how much milk is coming out. There's more on car pumping in Chapter 11.
- Don't let it get too far away from you. If breastfeeding is a major priority, tell people that. If you let three, four, or five days go by without getting in the time you need, you may find yourself hurting your supply as well as resenting your employer. It takes consistent effort to fit in the pumping sessions that you need.
- That said, don't stress over one missed or shortened session (or more). One bad day will not ruin your supply.
- Get creative with your schedule. One teacher I talked to said her principal scheduled all of her classes in a row, so she could get home to her baby as soon as possible. Others reduce their hours

in order to get the space needed to continue breastfeeding. Negotiating telecommuting for some or all workdays during breastfeeding can work for some jobs. Some women are able to have a caregiver bring the baby to the office for feedings.

- Try feeding your baby at her daycare (or whatever your childcare situation is) right as you drop her off, and right when you pick her up. Some women who don't respond well to the pump or who can't fit in a lot of pumping sessions while at work use this tactic to shave one or more pumping sessions off of their schedules.

- Remember that it (usually) gets better. The first few weeks are hardest, as you navigate the work environment, miss your baby, and try to train yourself and others on your new reality. The stress and awkwardness is likely to diminish. People will learn, one way or another, what pumping is, and why and when you need to do it. The number of pumping sessions you need to do may drop, too, as your baby begins to eat solid food and spaces out bottles or feedings at the breast.

- Go ahead, lose it every once in a while, whatever "losing it" looks like to you: having a good cry, getting mad and venting to your spouse, or gently taking it out on a sympathetic co-worker. You don't have to be perfect or amazing at this.

The Four Co-worker Types

Of those co-workers who interact with you enough to know that you are pumping breastmilk during the day, you have four types:

1. The Resentful One

   The Resentful One refers to your maternity leave as your "vacation." He is annoyed you are stepping away to pump. Quiet ones stew on this resentment, and it surfaces in other ways. Vocal ones loudly ask why everyone doesn't get multiple breaks in the day.

2. The Inappropriate Comment-Maker

   This person is uncomfortable with the knowledge that your breasts make milk and masks his discomfort with awkward jokes ("Save some for your husband's morning coffee!"), hand motions ("milking the cow" is a favorite), and questions ("So, are you going to keep doing that until the kid's in college?").

3. The "I'd Rather Not Know" Guy

   This person will not complain and will not bother you. He just wants to be left out of it. This is fine. You don't need every co-worker to be your ally. As long as this person is not overdoing the "I don't want to know" shtick to the point of it being attention-seeking, this is a perfectly fine role to play.

4. The Best Thing That Has Happened Since You Went Back to Work

   I don't know of a single woman who has survived pumping at work without a few of these people scattered around. These folks tend to exhibit some key traits:

   - They understand the basics of what's about to happen, or they're willing to learn.

- They ask you how they can help. If someone does this, take her seriously. Read this list to her, put her on your mental list of allies, and go back to her when you need help. And buy her a drink after work, ASAP.
- They keep snacks at their desk, and do not use the "breastmilk burns 500 calories a day" fact to ask you why you have not yet lost all of your baby weight.
- They offer up their office or car.
- They shut down bad-mouthers and inappropriate people. Sometimes you're just not going to fight those battles yourself.
- They come up with code language for when you really need to excuse yourself. Meetings run long, or people announce that "we're all going to work through lunch"—and your blood runs cold, because you know you're not going to make it all the way through. When you use your code word, these people do everything they can to get you out of the situation and to your pump. "I could really use a short break," they announce, and suddenly, they're a superhero.
- They assume you're still great at your job, and look for reasons to confirm that, rather than noticing the odd bad day to judge that you simply can't hack it.

Clueless People, Jerks, and Awkward Interrupters

Whether you have a workplace full of resentful people or living saints, you will find yourself in awkward situations with your co-workers on occasion. For example, you'll feel your boobs getting fuller and some person will be chatting away at you, oblivious to your pain. In these situations, you'll have to decide whether to shoot the person straight ("I have to go pump for a few minutes"), or draw on an arsenal of excuses ("Oh my goodness I just realized I'm late for a conference call / I have low blood sugar and am starting to feel woozy / I'm so sorry but I've just *got* to go to the restroom") to get out of there.

> Melissa was made partner at her law firm right after her maternity leave. Her firm has a tradition that the new partner hangs out in the hall all day with co-workers coming by to give congratulations. She had to duck into her office to pump and had people pounding on her door trying to get in.

> Janet, a counselor at a small college with few young mothers on staff, found that even though she put "personal time" on her calendar, people in her office were used to being able to drop by, and it was awkward to try to explain why she needed to stop chatting and close the door. More awkward? "Explaining to student workers what 'personal time' meant."

Denise was sometimes the only person in the office, so she would have to walk to the front of the office to let clients in, with her nursing cover still on.

Candace, an HR manager, had multiple instances of being locked in her office, with her CEO knocking on her door and not taking the hint when she shouted that she was busy and would come find him when she finished. "I couldn't stand to tell him what I was really doing," she remembered.

Jessica, a fundraiser, spilled breastmilk on her keyboard at her desk: "An email went out to the whole staff, stating, 'Some of our staff members have had accidents involving company equipment. The equipment can be destroyed by liquid spills (including breastmilk). Repeated accidents may result in employees paying for the items that have been destroyed.'"

Jen, a consultant, had bladder issues post-baby. She once had to run to a meeting from pumping, and literally wet her pants en route.

And most of us will be dialed into a conference call at some point, when someone on the line asks, "Does anyone else hear that weird whooshing noise?"

You will also suffer your own personal anguish about whether people in the office can hear your pump, whether they are wondering what you're doing in there, and what they think about all of it. How you handle other people hearing (many rooms are not soundproof) or knowing what you are doing depends on your relationship with your co-workers and your opinion on pumping. If co-workers ask, it's most likely that they don't know what the sound is, or don't know how it all works, and are asking out of benign curiosity.

Think about people using the bathroom. No one asks, "What do you do in there?" No one is creeped out by the sound of toilets flushing. This is because everyone knows what it's used for. Think about how you can take away the mystery for others and the anxiety for you. Being clear takes some courage.

Be proactive about protecting your lactation space. Ask HR to put a lock on the door and to have it bookable (on Outlook or similar) only by nursing mothers. It's a lot more uncomfortable to kick someone out when your boobs are about to pop than to set the stage ahead of time.

I Can't Believe He Just Said That

Throughout this journey, you will face shocking comments and behaviors, from bosses and co-workers alike.

> Laura, a researcher, said that her boss said he was supportive until he asked, in her performance review, where she went

twice a day. Her response: "Pumping. You support that." His answer to that? "I support it, but you should be at your desk."

Emily, a doctor, noted, "While my boss was supportive of my decision, I did have a middle manager who was very rude . . . once she made me wait so long to pump that I leaked through breast pads, sports bra, T-shirt and scrub top. It was awful and still makes me cringe."

Alison, a lawyer, recounted, "A female partner told me that I could not continue to pump when I went to trial because she was not going to risk the jury hearing 'those awkward sounds' coming from a public restroom, and court 'was just not going to stop for me' every time I needed to pump."

Christina, a paralegal, felt a lot of pressure to not take extra time because of other women on staff who were always noting how much "break time" she was taking.

Samantha, a news producer, received numerous emails from HR in the nine months that she pumped, asking when she thought she would be done using that room "because other people also need to use it."

These intrusions seem to step up after the one-year mark, when some people decide that it has been "too long." After a certain point, and everyone's point is different, people will begin to question why you are still doing this. I'm not telling you to *listen* to these people—these are your choices. This is just a heads-up that it might happen.

My personal opinion: There is so much judgment about not breastfeeding long enough and about how "creepy" it is to breastfeed for too long. There seems to be an impossible window in which you've gotten it just right for everybody's comfort level—a good mother but not a weirdo. I say screw that. However long you breastfeed (or don't) is your business.

Your coping tactics for these comments and pressures depend on your personality, your work environment, and the power relationship with the person making the comment.

I tend to call these things out head-on (unless it's a super high-up person saying it, in which case I think up an awesome comeback later and kick myself for not using it in the moment). Some of the women I talked to used humor as a deflector, then went along their way. Many just kept their heads down, tried to let the comments roll off their backs, and did what they had to do. A few called the behavior out, or played dumb and talked very openly about pumping, and in the process made the other person feel really sheepish.

Some of these stories meet the definition of harassment. If you feel uncomfortable in the workplace, consider addressing the issue with a manager, supervisor, or HR. Many corporations also have ethics hotlines. How this stuff makes you feel is individual, and you should not have to brush it off if it is affecting you.

Whether you make a formal complaint or address these issues in another way, do keep in mind that this situation is, by definition, temporary. Meeting these things with anger doesn't always serve your goal of getting your job done and getting home to see your kid. That isn't to say you shouldn't stand up for yourself—by all means, if the situation demands it, speak your mind or go talk to someone who can help. Just remember that the person making the ridiculous comment most likely has never experienced what you're going through.

Use your precious energy wisely when you decide to go to bat: on those whose change in behavior will most positively impact you and any future mothers to come through the system.

Besides, whether they mean to or not, these awkward people will sometimes give you a hell of a good laugh.

Amy, a city planner, reviews architectural plans. She had to teach the fire department that a "pump room" for an office building isn't always for building mechanicals.

Sarah, a policy advisor, left her pump on her desk, and a co-worker came in and asked her, "Do you have asthma? Is this your breathing machine?"

Rachael, a marketing director, had a European exec ask her, in front of a room full of forty people, "Are you breastfeeding? How is it going?" She recalled, "Some women were horrified. I thought it was funny."

Emily, a lawyer, had to explain to her 63-year-old male boss why the law referred to the pumping room as the "Express Room," after he commented that "there isn't anything 'express' about it."

Other Pumping Mothers: Your Best Support System

If you are lucky enough to have other pumping mothers at work at the same time as you (I say "lucky" even though this means you might be jostling to use the lactation space), you can build a support system. These women can lend you pump parts if you forget them. They can answer questions, from plugged ducts to dealing with your boss. They can just straight up complain with you. Get their numbers in your phone so you can get to them by phone or text. This support system can be useful even if you never see these women.

Leslie installed a cork board in her lactation room and left a notebook and pens on top of the fridge. The pumping mothers kept up a conversation with paper tacked to the board. Some topics were practical: "I forgot my ice pack! Anyone have a spare I can use until tomorrow?" And some were sweet: "Welcome to your first day back at work! We are here for you."

A word of caution: For all the good of connecting with other pumpers, drama is also possible. There are a lot of hormones involved in a group of new mothers! I've heard of women accusing other women of stealing their milk, so head this off at the pass with super clear markings on bottles, bags, and parts. Drama about use of the room is possible, and if this starts to escalate, ask HR for their help in settling issues in a way that works for everyone involved.

Chapter 10:
Washing and Storing

One of the messiest aspects of this whole business is washing the damn parts (you are likely to develop even stronger language to describe them) and storing your milk during a typical workday (more on storing milk on the road in Chapter 12).

Your setup will determine how easy or difficult this process is—if you have that luxury pumping suite, go ahead and skip this chapter and spend the time hanging out with your baby. But most of us will, at some point, find ourselves walking across an office with pump parts that are dripping milk, bottles of freshly pumped milk (with or without caps, depending on how awake you were that morning), and an intense fear of running into a male co-worker.

Getting to the Sink and Fridge

You will feel like a smuggler, trying to get these goods across the office without detection. You will find yourself at a shared sink (bathroom, kitchen), washing your pump parts when the worst possible person walks into the room. You might obsess about the possibility of someone opening, or even *using*, your breastmilk from the fridge or freezer, no matter how clearly marked it is with your name.

Not that discretion can fully protect you. I was once walking from a storage closet (where I pumped, perched on boxes of samples) to the office kitchen with my milk safely inside an opaque bag. A young, enthusiastic guy in our office came bounding up to me: "Whatcha got in the bag?" And before I could do anything, he proceeded to open the bag and peer inside.

I decided to just let him do it and allow his nosiness to play out to its natural conclusion. I waited until he had the top of the bag completely open, and his nose in there, and then I smiled sweetly and answered loudly, "That's breastmilk. I just pumped it." He turned a deep shade of red, mumbled an apology, and walked away.

At any rate, there are, as with everything in this process, things you can do to make life a bit easier and less awkward.

Washing

We've been through this in the Preparation section, but it's worth repeating. You have a few options on how to approach washing.

1. Suck it up and wash the things out in the open. Most people won't ask you what they are.
2. Put them in a large Ziploc bag, zip it shut, put that bag inside something opaque, and throw the whole thing in the fridge between pumping sessions, so you don't have to wash them until the end of the day. This is my preferred option, no matter how chilly the parts are on my boobs.

Washing and Storing

3. Buy multiple sets of pump parts so you only use each set once per day, and wash them all every night. Store them in Ziploc bags inside your pump bag until the end of the day.
4. Buy pump part wipes or microwaveable steam-sterilizer bags.

You may be wondering not only what tactic to use, but actually how (and how well) you need to wash your pump parts between feedings. I cannot tell you what to do here—I can only report what I and others have been comfortable with. I take the approach that breastmilk is both clean and stable, and that full sterilizing is a "when I remember to do it, which means once a week or so" thing.

In a typical workday, many women stick with water, maybe a drop of soap, and a bottle brush (don't leave the brush in the office kitchen where some fool will use it to clean the tomato sauce out of his Tupperware). I am fine with just water from the tap, and making sure the milk has been washed out of all nooks and crannies (you especially want to focus on the little membranes, if your pump has them).

Storing

Storing milk is relatively self-explanatory but I'll remind you of your options here.

1. Office fridge/freezer.
   Buy an opaque, insulated lunch bag with a secure closure. Label it clearly. If you have an office lunch thief, he is likely to lose interest

quickly upon looking inside the bag. Another option is to label it as "BABY FOOD." It's true without having to use the word "breast" at the office, and it stops people from being grossed out, which is not a hassle you need to deal with.

2. Mini-fridge.

   Ask for or purchase a fridge for your office, cubicle, or lactation room. You can store your parts in here between pumping sessions, too. (If you can help it, don't leave milk in there overnight, in case an overzealous janitor unplugs it.)

3. Cooler.

   Bring a cooler every day, and store the milk at your desk.

Chapter 11:
Pumping in Strange Places

In 2010, just before Christmas, I had the amazing and gut-wrenching opportunity to go on a business trip to Nepal. My son, home with my husband, was five months old. On the way to the airport, I begged my best friend to turn around and take me home (a working mom herself, she knew her job was to ignore me and get me to the airport). So there I went, halfway around the world, with my boobs, my milk, and my pump for company.

In my most surreal moment, I found myself in the back of a moving Land Rover en route to the birthplace of the Buddha. I was traveling with co-workers and a camera crew. I was wrapped in a shawl, hooked up to a breast pump (with a battery pack), and pumping breastmilk as we jostled our way down the road.

Everyone in that car (designated "ladies only") and the car in front of us knew what I was doing. When I finished pumping, I unhooked the pump and dumped the milk out the window of the moving car (so much for liquid gold).

Sometimes I still can't believe that this actual scenario happened to me. Everything about it was so . . . weird.

Throughout this trip, every moment that I was awake, I was scouting for places and time to pump. My short list of where I pumped (and dumped—there was no way to safely store milk and bring it home on that trip, and local clinics wouldn't accept donated milk) almost 300 ounces of milk in one of the strangest weeks of my life:

- A bathroom with no stalls or door, in the tiny domestic airport in Lumbini, Nepal. I got stuck at the airport due to a delay caused by the imminent arrival of the Queen Mother of Bhutan, which isn't something that happens to me every day. I will forever be grateful to my boss for the loan of her iPod and noise-canceling headphones to give me something else to focus on.
- A Land Rover, with the Himalayas as a moving backdrop that I couldn't enjoy due to the extreme stress of pumping in a car full of people. Multiple times.
- Parked in a field near a community health clinic, with two boys on bicycles peering in the car windows. I have never loved my large travel shawl more than at that moment.
- Bathrooms and/or public benches in the airports of the following countries: Nepal, Qatar, Thailand, USA.
- Multiple airplane bathrooms, and, when I finally ran out of modesty and energy, my actual seat on the airplane.

This scenario might not mirror yours, but your situation doesn't have to be exotic to be stressful. My trip to Nepal was the reason I first started asking other women about their experiences with working and breastfeeding, and the catalyst to learning that, whether it's a dirt road in another time zone or a dusty storage closet with no electrical outlet, most working and breastfeeding mothers ending up pumping in strange places, and we all need help making it work.

Why You'll End up Somewhere Weird

Pumping in strange places is almost a given of business travel (see Chapter 12 for more on business trips and Chapter 13 for specific guidance on pumping in airports and airplanes), but there are plenty of other day-to-day reasons you might find yourself pumping somewhere less than ideal. These reasons range from the mundane (a long commute) to the supposedly glamorous (a news producer whose newscast always went on the air at the time she was supposed to be pumping).

For some women, it's just their everyday thing: pumping in the car because it's easier or better than whatever their employer has to offer, pumping in an on-call room at the hospital, sneaking in a few minutes in a precious loaner office with a door, pumping in a courthouse bathroom, or pumping huddled in a Pre-K classroom closet while holding the door shut with one hand.

> Maggie, a non-profit professional, had a meeting at a conference facility. She called ahead for a private place to pump. Upon her arrival, the facility manager was clueless (lesson: the message doesn't always make it to the right person), but brought Maggie to a conference room with floor-

to-ceiling windows facing a public walkway. Maggie protested and was then escorted to a locker room with no locking door. The staff promised her she'd be fine. Ten minutes later, the actual, real-life Harlem Globetrotters walked into the locker room and into the middle of Maggie's pumping session.

We pump milk in places we would never have imagined suitable to produce food for a baby. Places where our modesty and decency are constantly under threat. Places that cause us so much anxiety that our milk seems to go into hiding (oxytocin, which creates the letdown reflex, is easily blocked by stress). Places where we find ourselves fast-forwarding to the moment we can tell our girlfriends all about it.

You need to know about these weird pumping places so you can be prepared with the best ways to make them work, avoid the worst when possible, and not feel so alone when you find yourself perched in a bizarre location with only the rhythmic sound of your pump to keep you company.

Gear and Equipment for Strange Places

If you know you'll be pumping somewhere strange, start off with the stuff in your pumping bag, as listed in Chapter 2. Then add in the following, and pare down over time, to your own essentials:

1. A small pack of wet wipes for surfaces like your car dashboard or your briefcase.

2. Headphones and an mp3 player or phone loaded with music or podcasts. Some places you will pump are so terrible you will want to block them out with sound.
3. A "hooter hider," shawl, or similar cover-up, in case of unexpected walk-ins.
4. A flashlight app on your phone. In a closet or on the side of the road at night, the glow of your screen just isn't enough.
5. Paper and tape to cover a car or door window.
6. If you can fit it, a single-boob hand pump.

There are a few "weird pumping" locations that cover most situations. As stressful as it is to imagine yourself pumping in one of them, the good news is that we have blazed this trail before you, and we're here to tell you how to do it.

Car Pumping

I talked with dozens of women who use their cars to pump—on the commute, during the workday, or en route to client meetings, and they shared tricks that will make this experience much easier.

Covering up

Pumping in a car can make you feel very exposed. There are many ways to cover up depending on your situation and your level of modesty.

If you're pumping while driving (PWD), you need a good pumping bra and "hooter hider." Do not expect to feel discreet. As Carrie informed me, "Truck drivers can see you, regardless of what your husband says."

If you're parked, consider using a sunshade on the windshield. For windows, bring blankets or towels, crack the window, stuff the blanket in the crack, and roll the window back up for makeshift curtains.

Power

With a running car, you can use a car adapter for power, but be prepared that the power from your car can sometimes be erratic. If you're parked and don't want to run the car, you'll need a battery adapter. Always, always keep a spare value-sized pack of batteries nearby, and remember that on a lot of pumps the battery pack has two sides that need batteries.

Pumping While Driving (PWD)

Serious disclaimer: This can be dangerous if not done carefully. No amount of breastmilk is worth an accident. Follow all traffic laws!

There are some great upsides to PWD. First, you get more productive time at work because you don't have to pump right when you get there. Second, some women actually find this to be the most relaxing time to pump.

Shannon noted, "I loved pumping in the car to and from work. I was alone and it took my mind off pumping and how much milk I was getting. I wound up getting more because I wasn't focusing on it."

Obviously, there are some logistical challenges to making this work. Assembly is crucial to getting it right. Pumping while driving requires a truly hands-free set-up.

It works best if your pumping bottles are resting on your legs, rather than just hanging down, so that you don't have to steady or hold anything with your hands.

So first, get bigger pump bottles. For example, Medela pumps come with six-ounce bottles, but they also sell eight–to-ten ounce bottles, which are tall enough to rest on your thighs while you pump and drive. Some baby bottles also fit with some models of pump, so you could use, for example, a tall Dr. Brown's bottle or something similar.

Next, play around with seat positioning, which can impact your physical comfort and stability as well as how visible you feel. Try leaning your seat back or forward more than you're used to. Sometimes, moving the seat forward can make your knees bend more deeply, meaning your thighs are higher up, which might give you a better surface to rest those bottles on.

You need to start the pumping process *before* you start driving. Before you even turn the car on, make sure both cup holders are empty, put a towel on your lap, assemble your pump (with bottles—never bags in this setting), and get the horns into your bra.

Make sure everything is secured tightly: The horns have to be really "in there" in case you get jostled, and the tubes have to be really well plugged in. The tubes also have to be situated so any arm movements won't rip them out of their sockets. Put breast pads inside your bra, just below each horn, in case of leakage. Cover yourself with your nursing cover, and start the car.

If your drive is long enough that you'll need to stop pumping mid-drive, make sure you have very easy arm's reach to the plug or the "off" button on the pump, or pull over to turn it off. If you have to keep driving, you could drive onward with the pump parts hanging off your boobs. At this point of this particular drive, you have really said goodbye to both modesty and the cool factor. You could also pull over and get the milk into a cooler or put the bottles in the cup holders. If you won't be driving for hours on end, leaving the milk at car temperature is fine. (See Chapter 4 for more on storage times at various temperatures.) Don't let anyone rush you while taking the flanges out of your bra—the last thing you want is spilled milk because someone honked their horn when the light turned green.

Guerrilla Pumping

If you have a job that keeps you on the road a lot and you don't like the PWD option, do some creative mapping ahead of time. Get familiar with the location of all the Babies 'R' Us locations and any maternity stores in your area. Those folks will usually let you pump in the store. Learn where the more private roadside pull-offs, scenic overlooks, and parking garages are located. Figure out which stores have those wonderful family restrooms (often with an electrical outlet) that you can lock yourself in. And be prepared to PWD, just in case.

Closet Pumping

A storage closet might be your everyday reality, or it might be your occasional go-to when meeting offsite or inadvertently locked out of your normal pumping space at your own office. Be forewarned that it will not feel fun or relaxing to be hunched over in a dark, small, windowless place—and often without an electrical outlet or a lock.

> Amy, a literary agent, pumped in a closet that housed her office's shared printer. "Whenever I heard the printer start up," she said, "I knew I had about two minutes until some guy started banging on the door—despite my Do Not Disturb sign—demanding his printed stuff."

Once you find a place to set your pump (this could be the floor, your knees, a box, or a filing cabinet) and sort out a power option, your biggest concern will be making sure the door stays shut, which might require you keeping one hand on the door handle while you pump.

If closet pumping is your norm, you and this closet are going to become close friends, so try to make some modifications for comfort and privacy. You might want to "liberate" a chair from elsewhere in the office to live inside the closet, so you don't have to sit on top of boxes or on the floor. You could hang a tension curtain rod and a shower or cloth curtain across the inside of the door frame, so that if the door is opened, you've bought yourself a few extra seconds to yell, "Occupied! Close the door!" With permission (or without it, depending on how much of a badass you want to be), you could even install a combination lock on the inside of the door.

If a closet isn't a regular pumping place that you can plan for and protect, you might have less ability to prepare and to control whether someone can open the door. Consider a sign, taped just above eye level, reading "OCCUPIED—DO NOT OPEN." Keep covered up inside the closet, so an unexpected intrusion is not as horrible as it could be. (It'll still be at least a little bit horrible.)

Pumping in Another Building in Your Office Complex

I was actually shocked at how many women I talked to whose employers assigned them a lactation room in another building and expected the whole process, including the walk to and from the other building, to fit into a 15-to-20-minute window.

Samantha was a news producer when she had her baby, and her desk was in a common workspace on the TV news set. HR assigned her a pumping room in another building. She'd grab her pumping bag and cooler, and run—literally run—over to the other building. She would then take an elevator up seven floors, unlock the door to the dirty, un-cleaned office, and set up. Once hooked up, she'd be back on email with reporters, discussing the next newscast. She gave herself fifteen minutes to pump, regardless of whether she felt done or not. Then the pump parts went, unwashed, into a Ziploc bag and into the cooler, and she'd sprint back to the other building, with her pump and cooler in tow, and get back to work. The whole process took about thirty minutes.

If your pumping space requires a mini-commute, you'll need to become an efficiency expert. Store your pump parts in a Ziploc bag in a fridge or cooler—it's sanitary and saves the washing time. (As I've noted, when you go to pump again, these chilled parts will feel refreshing, a.k.a. really cold, on your boobs. If you have sore breasts from pumping and breastfeeding, sometimes it can actually feel nice. But mostly, it's just shockingly cold.) Bring your phone with you so you can work on the walk over and back, or even while pumping.

If this commute isn't working, consider looking for a closet, asking a kind co-worker to borrow his or her private office, or making friends at other companies in the building; they might have more enlightened HR departments. In buildings housing multiple businesses, there may be extra rooms, such as unoccupied closets or offices, and it's worth asking the building management company for access. If none of these is an option, consider whether you can actually get to your car faster than walking to a far-away pumping space.

Sharing Space with Other Pumpers

In an office without a lactation room, mothers often find each other and scheme ways to make pumping work. If you can't work around each other's schedules, sync up your pumping schedules so you can be each other's lookouts, defenders, problem-solvers, curtain-hangers, and it's-time-to-talk-to-HR buddies. Nursing mothers tend to drop their modesty around each other pretty quickly, so you can also, in a tiny space like a closet, set up chairs back-to-back and pump in tandem.

Someone Else's Turf

Sales calls. Conferences. Meetings with clients or vendors. You might find yourself in someone else's office building for a wide variety of reasons.

This situation can significantly up the awkward factor, or, if you're the who-cares type, it could relieve you of all your modesty since you don't have to see these people every day. When you do pump offsite, it could be in any of the situations described in this chapter—a car, a closet, a bathroom, an office, a conference room, and so on. In any case, you will have to figure out location, washing parts, and storing milk in a new setting.

The best thing you can do is call ahead. Find a female receptionist or assistant and explain your situation. You will feel more comfortable talking to a woman. Tell her you need help finding a room to pump in for X minutes, Y times while you are there. Tell her you will also need access to a fridge or freezer. See if she'll give you her cell phone number so you can find her when you get there. Buy a small gift card to bring her as a thank-you. When you arrive, find this nice lady first.

If you can't call ahead, make it a priority to find an ally as soon as you arrive. The receptionist or the woman with pictures of her baby on her desk are good bets. If all of the people at this location are unhelpful, prepare to pump in the bathroom (more on that below).

Public Restrooms

Wherever you are—in an airport, at your own or a client's office, at a conference—if you cannot get into an actual room or a family restroom with its locking door, counter space, and electrical outlet (finding one of these is a small victory for many pumping women, and it's always worth asking if one is available), you are going to find yourself facing down one of the worst pumping locales of all: sitting on a toilet in a public bathroom stall. There is truly no way to make this situation wonderful, but a few tricks exist to make it slightly less terrible:

- Before you go into the stall, grab some paper towels. Toilet paper falls apart too easily when wet, and you might need to clean up spills.
- My favorite trick comes from Jenny, who discovered that by placing a Post-it Note over the automatic flush sensor, she could stop the toilet from flushing on her (clothed) butt every few minutes.
- You might find yourself in a particularly disgusting location, where you don't want to sit on the toilet, let alone pump milk. If a place like this is ever your lot in life, hang your pump from the coat hook on the inside of the stall door. Remain standing to pump. Hang your pump horns inside your bra. Keep your music player handy, get your earbuds in, close your eyes, and play that thing as loud as you can.
- Your well-stocked pump bag becomes critical in the bathroom, because everything you need has to be accessible, probably with only one hand, while hanging on that hook on the back of the bathroom door.
- If you're not the hang-up-and-stand type, you will still need to decide where to put your pump—your choices are the floor, your knees, on top of your suitcase/briefcase, or the tiny metal shelf that is sometimes available. The top of that horrible little feminine products garbage can is not a viable option.
- If you are in an airport, you might worry that people will hear the sound and think you're making a bomb in there (I once developed this neurosis in the Bangkok airport in the middle of

the night). The only real solution here is to try to put this thought out of your mind. Remember that most people are trying to block out other people's bathroom sounds, regardless of why they're making them.

- You will have to make your own call about whether to wash your pump parts in the bathroom sink. I don't—I buy a bottle of water and rinse, or if it's my last or even second-to-last time pumping for the day, I just throw the parts in a Ziploc bag without washing them.

Pumping in Your Private Office

If you have an office with a door, you can shut the door, relax, and do your business. Right? Yes, but your office has its own considerations.

Pumping while on the phone

Whoever you're talking to will likely hear your pump. You can only get the machine so far away from your body, of course, so experiment with different ways to muffle the sound—throw a blanket over the pump or stuff a sweater into the opening where the actual machinery sits. If the person on the other end asks, "What's that sound?", lie like your life depends on it. Play dumb ("I don't hear anything! Maybe it's on your end?"), invent a construction scenario right outside your window, or blame a poor connection.

People barging in

In an office where people don't tend to close their doors, it can be awkward to explain to people (especially male co-workers and higher-ups) why you need your door closed and locked.

> Katie got some nearby construction workers to cut a plywood board that she could stick in the door to keep it from opening. After a while, the board also served as a visual cue to co-workers that Katie's office was temporarily off-limits.

Your office, while the envy of pumping women, may not always be the safe haven it seems. Look into getting a lock if you don't have one, even a makeshift variety.

Glass

You might have a glass door or windows into the office, and don't forget the windows to the outside world: take it from Ann, who had a close encounter with a window washer. Talk to HR about frosting the glass or hanging curtains, or get tension rods and hang your own.

Non-Desk Workplaces

Much of making a "non-desk" environment work comes down to the strange places listed above. When you're constantly on the go, with no desk as home base to stash stuff and no friendly storage closet to call your own, extra skills and strategies are required.

> Tracy, a news producer, spends much of the day in the studio where her show is filmed. She set up a system where she emailed the Operations person to find an empty office or dressing room to pump in. This would take about an hour to confirm, so she would start the process early.

> Erin works in home care, driving from house to house, so she mapped out where all the Babies 'R' Us stores were because they were a friendly place to pump.

> Ellen, another news producer, works on a news magazine show. On her second day back from leave, she had to produce an interview with a well-known celebrity and a demanding on-air correspondent. She had thirty minutes before they were going to roll, so she thought she had plenty of time to pump. Suddenly, her correspondent and interview subject walked into the room and said, "We're ready." She panicked—her boobs were rock hard and already leaking. She sneaked out and missed the first twenty minutes of the interview (an enormous no-no as a producer, but you gotta do what you gotta do).

I talked with women in almost every walk of professional life: political operatives on the campaign trail, electricians on construction sites, detectives on the police force, bartenders, and more. They consistently brought up three survival strategies:

- If you're on the road, know your routes and safe places (and get good at pumping while driving).
- If you have a predictable schedule, build allies and plan way ahead.
- When everything else fails, wing it, and prepare to ask forgiveness rather than permission.

For me, one of the most helpful techniques in my journey of pumping in many strange places was just knowing that so many women had done this before me, and were doing it with me, so to speak. There's a masochistic sorority made up of women who pump at work. In my experience, there's no one-upmanship—we are not trying to outdo each other with our crazy stories. There is, instead, a desire to laugh and cry together over the lengths we have gone to in order to keep providing breastmilk to our babies. None of this is particularly fun, but there is a real badge of honor that goes with the territory, and while most people will never know what you did (and where you did it) for your baby, your fellow working mothers know, and we salute you for it.

So . . . go forth, working mama. Pump your milk in strange places. Get mad about it if you need to. Text your girlfriends while it's happening to share in your misery. Remember that you're doing this for your kid, and the thought of that little person just might get you through until you're home, holding that baby (and/or a glass of wine), and remembering why you put yourself through such craziness.

Section 3: Business Travel

Just when you've got everything figured out, your first business trip, conference, or offsite day with clients rears its head. Business travel breeds a particular type of anxiety because it has so many new variables and unknowns. The first trip is almost always the hardest, and with the tips in this section you can quickly become a battle-hardened road warrior.

Chapter 12: Doing Your Business on a Business Trip

At home base, maybe you've got the pumping thing down to a science. You know where you pump every day—even if it's in your car or a supply closet—and you have your gear and your system. Then the dreaded business trip arrives. You now have the pain of leaving your baby, coupled with the joy of a great night's sleep and the stress of how to pump in a new environment.

This chapter will focus on how to make allies, deal with hotels, and find pumping locations while on the road. Its companions are Chapters 11 and 13. Chapter 11 provides details on how to make unusual pumping locations work, since business travel might force you to pump in closets, in trains/planes/automobiles, and sitting on toilets in public restrooms. Chapter 13 covers specifics of air travel and how to transport milk back home.

> MaryAnn, a research scientist, recounted the business trip pumping story that still makes her sweat: "I had a last-minute meeting in a hotel. I stepped out to find a place to pump because I was dying, and the young, male concierge just couldn't figure it out. After a conversation that left us both beet red, he found a room for me: the executive Board of Directors

conference room with floor-to-ceiling windows and wall-to-wall flat-screens. Not at all convinced I wasn't being observed by all of the security and monitoring equipment I know existed in that room, I hunkered down in a corner and pumped as fast as I could. I told myself that I would never again doubt my dedication as a provider to my son."

Amy, a railroad employee, pumped on a trip to China, in bathrooms with no running water, pick-up trucks next to railroad tracks, and hotels and restaurants.

Cindy, a doctor, talked about "the pain of pump and dump on the road when there is no freezer available."

Ali, a lawyer, had to explain to security in a Mexican airport why she needed to travel with milk when she didn't have her baby with her.

Supply: The Goal of Pumping on a Work Trip

I want you to prepare yourself for the possibility that, when you go on a business trip, your pumped milk may not make it back home with you. It could spill or leak. You could run out of luck finding a fridge or freezer. You might produce less because your schedule is bound to be screwy, from flight or train times to time in the car or in the air to the busy-ness of being offsite.

So, repeat after me: the #1, #2, and #3 reasons to pump on a business trip are to *maintain supply, avoid plugged ducts, and avoid engorgement.* Somewhere down the list is bringing milk back home, but it is *not* the primary goal. If you return from a trip having more or less maintained your supply, but with a diminished freezer stash at home, you have been totally successful on your trip, period.

Making Friends

No matter what your destination is, finding an ally helps. A lot. Ahead of time, find a female receptionist, assistant, HR person, or office manager, and make her your ally. Get her phone number and figure out how to find her when you get to the office, conference center, or other destination. Consider purchasing a small thank-you gift for her. Ask if any women in the office are new mothers, and get introduced to them. If no one there is familiar with breastfeeding, explain that you need to pump milk and will need a private space with a locking door to pump for twenty minutes at a time. They will help you find a room. They will show you the sink and fridge. And they will help you feel so much less stressed out about the whole thing. If you try to make friends with someone who turns out to be a jerk, move on and find a new friend. Pumping on the road is all about stubbornly keeping at it until you get what you want.

If you'll be at a conference facility, call ahead and ask whether there is a nursing mother's room or a room you can use to pump. Ask where in the facility it is and how to get access to it. If it is far away, start to plan back-ups, like your rental car or the bathroom.

Traveling with Co-workers or Clients

There's no easy way around this aspect of business travel while breastfeeding. Most travel makes for close quarters, be it in a car, an airport, an airplane, or a conference room. No matter how awkward it might be, I swear to you that it will just be easier to bite the bullet and tell any co-workers or clients you are in transit with that you are breastfeeding, you have some weird gear with you, and you will have to disappear a couple of times a day. Otherwise you might find yourself, like Erin, in an airport security line when a male co-worker informed her she had "something" leaking from her bag.

Storing Your Milk in a Hotel

Most business travel involves a hotel stay, so you need to think about where you will be storing your milk overnight. Call your hotel ahead of time and ask for a room fridge with a freezer compartment (that tiny freezer actually will freeze a couple of bags of milk overnight). Tell them it's for medical purposes. If they say no, say "medical purposes" again, and ask to speak to a manager. I am normally a truthful person, but I once had such a disagreeable hotel employee to deal with that I told him I was diabetic and needed the fridge for my medicine. That did the trick. However you accomplish it, if they agree to give you a fridge, call again the morning of your check-in to re-confirm this.

Some hotel staff will tell you to use the minibar fridge, which is fine, except that those fridges are full of minibar stuff and the newer ones have sensors that charge you if something is moved from its spot. When you're checking in, tell the person at reception that if you're going to use the minibar fridge, say it with me now, For Medical Purposes, you will have to move items out, you will return them before you check out, and you expect not to be charged for any of them.

If they absolutely won't budge on giving you a fridge, get them to agree—preferably in writing with a manager's signature, so you can prove it to the late-night desk person who will inevitably claim he was never informed of such an arrangement—to let you store a small, labeled bag of medicine (the word "medicine" freaks people out way less than "breastmilk") in the employee or kitchen freezer every night. Put your milk in an opaque bag and label it with your name, phone number, room number, and "MEDICINE: DO NOT OPEN." March it down to the front desk, smile brightly, and get that milk where it needs to go. Ask the person to confirm where it is going so you know how to describe its location to another employee. Plan for a few extra minutes in the morning when you need to retrieve it since there will be a different person on duty who is sure to have no idea what you're talking about.

International Pumping

Not everyone will have the experience of traveling internationally, without the baby, while still breastfeeding. I don't really wish it on anyone. The separation from the baby is hard enough, but even if you enjoy the new scenery, there's no real "break" due to the demands of pumping, and pumping in far-flung places has its own set of challenges.

Not all international experiences will be as crazy as my Nepal story, but wherever you're headed, you should still do a lot of planning, and prepare to power through some unpleasant stuff. It is stressful. It is hard work. But it is doable. You will come home exhausted, but feeling like a badass for having made it work. And oh, the stories you will be able to tell your girlfriends.

When traveling internationally, think about the power system before you go and bring the right adapters. If the power supply is in any way unreliable, use batteries. Burning out your pump motor from a power surge is not in your best interest.

Travel Gear

Everything we've already gone over in terms of gear still holds. Refer to your lists in Chapters 2 and 11, and then, when going on a business trip, keep the following in the front of your mind:

- For your first trip, bring everything—in future trips you'll know what works for you and can pare down.

- Bring more breastmilk storage bags than you think you will need and a Sharpie to label them.
- Bring a cooler bag. Remember that a lunch-sized bag will work for a one- to two-day trip, and something that would hold a six-pack will work for three days to a week.
- Do not skimp on the large Ziploc bags.
- Bring your hand pump in your carry-on luggage. Business travel usually makes for busier days—especially when you have a baby at home and are trying to keep the trip as short as possible. You might find that you sometimes can only get a quick pump in.
- Double check that you have your pump, bottles, parts, power cord (no kidding—check), battery pack, and extra batteries. Then check again.
- Bring that big shawl, which will be cover, noise-muffler, and lifesaver.
- Pack back-up clothes if you will not have access to laundry. The last thing you need is to run out of clothes because they all smell of spilled breastmilk.

Chapter 13:
The Mile-High Milk Club

Picture this: you're on your way home from a business trip, having successfully pumped and frozen several bags full of breastmilk. You have figured out how to make a breast pump, a cold bag filled with frozen milk, your laptop, your purse, and everything else with you look like "one carry-on and one personal item." And now you're at security. So, what do you do when a rumpled TSA agent (who, just before you walked up, touched his 1,000th traveler of the day without washing his hands) wants to open a bag of your frozen breastmilk and wave a little test slip of paper in there?

Air travel plus breastmilk can seem like a daunting task, especially the first time, but it's doable. So I'm going to break this down into its simple parts.

First, remember that frozen milk absolutely can survive a plane trip or a long car or train trip.

Second, remember what I said in the previous chapter: on a business trip, you have got to look at the milk you bring back home as "bonus" milk. Expect to lose some (or all) along the way to leakage and temporarily diminished supply due to the stress of travel. Don't let it kill you to lose some, and remember that you can always make more.

Third, remember it is your *legal right* to fly with breastmilk.

Packing for the Plane

Business travel means carry-ons—be it your overnight bag, your computer, or your purse. Pumping means even more carry-ons, especially on the way home when you are lugging milk with you. This is a juggling act, but it's doable.

Some women say that they get around the "one carry-on and one personal item" rule by telling TSA that the pump is "medical equipment." If you can do this, more power to you, but it made me too nervous to risk it. TSA is such a crapshoot—everything depends on the agent you get at that moment. It's a good idea to pack as if this were not an option, just in case you encounter an ornery TSA agent who doesn't believe in the "medical equipment" thing and won't budge.

Plan to give up your purse for the flight. If you want a purse on your trip, pack it into your suitcase and put the essential purse items into your pump bag or your other carry-on.

> Emily told me, "I used to jam a small bag with makeup, travel brush, and other toiletry items down one side of the pump bag, and my wallet, keys, and phone down the other side."

When packing to leave for your trip, mentally prepare for the cooler bag of milk you'll be bringing home. This cooler bag, if you can't fit it into something else, counts as a carry-on, so practice filling it with bags of frozen or liquid milk and cramming it into the top of the pump bag or your other carry-on. Even if you have stuff spilling out of the top, if you can make it look like two bags of the appropriate size, you're good. No one said the two carry-ons have to look good.

Finally, in preparation, plan to put all of your pump parts into Ziploc bags before you get to the airport. Some TSA agents will insist on taking everything out of your pump bag, and you do not want them touching your pump parts.

Pumping in the Airport

Pumping at the airport is generally preferable to pumping on the airplane, if your schedule allows it, because you can have more space and more privacy. Wherever you pump in the airport, set an alarm on your phone so you don't miss your flight.

> Chelsea, a lawyer, told me that she was mid-pump in an airport bathroom when her boss called her and told her the flight had started boarding. She turned off the pump, dumped the milk (because she didn't have time to bag it), and sprinted for the plane . . . only to find the doors had already closed.

Airports can actually be fine places to pump, provided you can find and commandeer a "family restroom" (or, if you have the points, the airline's executive lounge). Family restrooms beat the pants off sitting on a toilet seat in a regular stall.

What is great about these rooms is that they often have counters (to rest the pump and bottles), sinks, and electrical outlets. These bathrooms feel like they were made for pumping, so I do not feel guilty about taking one over for twenty minutes. It's a family restroom, and you're doing this for your family. If you cannot get a family restroom, or feel too nervous to take one over, go back to Chapter 11 for pointers on pumping in a public bathroom. However, be aware that family restrooms are not fool-proof (in pumping, nothing really is).

> Karen, a web development executive, once found herself shouting "Occupied!" and fending off someone knocking on the family restroom door. After ten minutes, a police officer appeared outside the restroom and demanded to be let in. Karen complied, opening the door with her shirt still unbuttoned, and declared: "I. Am. Pumping. Milk. For. My. Baby." The officer apologized and left.

Something similar happened to me in the San Francisco airport. I was going straight to a black-tie event, so I had to pump and throw on a dress in the airport before doing my makeup in a taxi. I had just started pumping in the family restroom when a lady started pounding on the door. The woman was in a wheelchair and didn't think I should be using that facility. I felt terrible, and kept asking her to please wait.

(Fun fact: being shouted at by an angry stranger is not a relaxing activity to help with letdown!) When I did come out, she angrily asked me where my baby was, revealing a deep lack of understanding as to why I would pump breastmilk in an airport bathroom in the first place.

Pumping on an Airplane

Of all the ways to pump, this is not one of the fun ones, but it's doable. When I say "doable," I don't mean "comfortable," "fun," or "something I'll look back on fondly later." It is none of these things. But what we are shooting for is doable. After all, you're in an enclosed space miles above the ground, with very little room to maneuver. The bathrooms are impossibly small just for the act of peeing (who has sex in these things, and why?). You are packed into a tiny space with a lot of people, none of whom you want seeing your boobs or smelling breastmilk. So . . . how do you do it?

- Plan ahead. Book a window seat, and try to get an empty row. Check www.seatguru.com to see which seats have electrical outlets. Do not book a seat next to your co-worker, unless you're really comfortable with that person.
- Wear layers to allow for easy access and modesty. A good combo is a camisole with a shirt and cardigan on top.
- Bring that big shawl.
- Buy a bottle of water after you clear security.

Now you have two options. The first is to pump in the bathroom on the plane. The second is to pump at your seat. No, I'm not kidding.

Pumping in the airplane bathroom is your more modest option, but it's also much less comfortable. If you're super calm and collected, you'll find that if you are casual about it, it isn't a big deal to anyone else. But if you're like me, you will probably worry about flight attendants and fellow passengers thinking you've died or are doing something illegal in there.

If the latter is you, your first job is to find a friendly flight attendant and make him or her your ally. "I'm a new mom and I'm traveling without my baby, and I could really use your help," is a good way to start. It is your call on whether to target the older, motherly type; the young man who will be flustered and therefore want to help you just to make it stop; or the woman who might have a baby of her own. I learned this step the hard way my first time, when I was holed up in the airplane bathroom with a worried (male) flight attendant knocking on the door asking me if I was okay because I had been in there for fifteen minutes already. Tell this person that you need to pump breastmilk in the bathroom, and that you didn't want them to think you'd fallen in or something. And then go and do it.

Get in there with your battery pack, your bottle of water, your wipes, your cold bag, and some music or a magazine. Sit on the toilet with the lid down. Balance the pump on your knees or put it on the minuscule counter (which is probably wet). You will know how to do the rest. Afterwards, rinse out the pump parts with your bottled water (don't use the sink water), cap your pump bottles, and clean up any spilled milk with the wipes. Worry about a full wash of the pump parts once you're on the ground.

Pumping in your airplane seat is your other option. I don't imagine anyone will do this on their first rodeo, but many veteran business-tripping moms totally go there.

Katie assured me, "The pump is not audible over the noise of the plane. Most people don't notice what you are doing, and if they do, they probably don't care. And if they do care, you shouldn't. You're doing a great thing for your baby."

I finally bit the bullet on an international flight. After squeezing myself and my equipment into too many airplane bathrooms, I found myself on a flight to Qatar (less glamorous than it sounds) and just done with the whole thing. The lights were down on the plane, and most people were already fast asleep, riding the Ambien train. I had no seatmates in my row, and the white noise of the airplane seemed loud enough to mask my pump's sounds.

I threw my essential travel shawl over myself, set everything up discreetly, and pumped while watching a *30 Rock* re-run on the seatback TV. I swear to you that no one noticed. Or if they did, I didn't know, and didn't want to know.

You can do this. Just swaddle yourself, peek down as you get yourself set up, and let 'er rip. Once you're done, you can still go into the bathroom and wash out your parts with bottled water or just throw them in a Ziploc bag and deal with it on solid ground.

Clearing Security with Milk in Tow

On your way back home, you will need to think about clearing your milk (frozen and/or liquid) through airport security.

> Liz, a researcher, was coming back from a conference with three days' worth of milk as a carry-on. The TSA agent was a really cute young man, and both Liz and "the poor guy" were blushing the whole time he pulled out each milk bag. To make matters worse, her co-workers were watching from the sidelines, cracking up laughing.

> Tracy, a journalist, ran the gamut of TSA experiences: "The first few times they tested the milk differently. One time, they opened a bottle and waved a strip over the open mouth. The other time, they put it in a machine. I protested the machine and had to speak to a manager to avoid it, since I didn't know what it would do to the milk."

One option is to pack your milk into your checked luggage. There, your milk will be safe from the curiosity of TSA agents. This option is most viable when you are flying direct, so you don't have to stress about your bag being somewhere warm during the layover. But this option carries the risk of your bag being delayed or lost, which could result in you losing all of that milk.

If you decide to carry on (which I always do), your first step is to allow for extra time. Not everyone experiences delays—I usually breeze through, for whatever reason—but stuff happens.

April noted, "When I bring milk, it's a guaranteed search and questioning. They take apart everything in the bag and look through it. One thing that speeds up the process on the front end of the trip is if I enter security with no milk, then pump in the airport bathroom once I'm through security."

Your second step is to pack your milk into your cooler bag. If you have a decent amount of frozen milk, the bags act as ice packs to each other, so you don't even necessarily need an actual ice pack. But if you have room, throw an ice pack or two in there. You can purchase the gel kind that hold their coldness longer than ice made from water.

Pack the milk bags in double heavy-duty Ziploc bags in case of leaks, and then into the cooler. Use Ziploc bags so liberally you start to wonder if you're keeping the company in business. (By this point, you already own stock in a company that sells big shawls . . . right?) You want to do anything possible to avoid leaking—because you don't want to lose the milk and you don't want to spend several travel hours smelling of breastmilk. If you have liquid milk, keep it in bottles to avoid spilling, if possible, and try to use an ice pack.

Third, when you get to the airport, remember that, in the United States, you are allowed to bring as much breastmilk through security as you want. It is food for your baby, regardless of whether or not your baby is there. When you get to security, say to the attendant, "I am a nursing mother and I'm traveling with a breast pump and breastmilk." If it's all frozen, say so, because that often makes things easier. In the best cases, they'll just wave you on, or they might even call someone over to walk you through security—the best kind of VIP (very important pumper?) treatment.

Whatever happens next, don't let that milk out of your sight.

The rules on what TSA can and can't do to your milk at security are frustratingly vague. For the record, TSA's website (as of 2014) lists breastmilk as part of the category of "liquid medications" (whether or not you are traveling with your baby). This means you can ask for the milk not to be put through an x-ray machine—but if you do make this request, they can subject it to "further inspection" (no further explanation is given, leaving the question open for argument, which is never a good idea with TSA). Because breastmilk is considered a medication, this means you can bring ice packs to keep it cool.

Some officers will just wave milk through. Others will want to put one unopened bag in a machine (which I let them do, and my kids seem okay, most of the time). I have had people try to open a bag and wave some kind of sensor in it, and I have absolutely put my foot down, and won. I have also seen them run that little cloth wipe thingy around the inside of my pump bag to test it for explosives.

Emily had the experience of bringing liquid milk home, and a male TSA agent insisting on putting a test strip into each bottle of milk. "He was doing everything he could not to gag while putting the test strips in," she says, "and he seemed especially grossed out by the warm bottle, which I had pumped five minutes before going through security."

While the TSA language, as of 2014, says that an officer may ask you to open a container during the screening process, it does not say that they are allowed to open it themselves, or that they are allowed to do anything to it once it's open. I don't know if this gives me a leg to stand on, but I tell them that if they open it, my doctor says I will have to throw it away, and this is food that my baby needs as soon as I land. I keep in my back pocket the lie (which I am not proud of) that my baby is allergic to anything but my breastmilk, so this milk is necessary to keep him alive.

I also print out the page from the TSA website (see Chapter 19 for a link) so I can wave it around if I need to. Most TSA agents don't know enough to challenge that, and invoking paperwork makes them nervous. If necessary, escalate to a supervisor and/or try to cry.

A note on international travel: Different countries have their own rules on bringing breastmilk onto the plane. Do your homework! If you are concerned about getting your milk taken away at security in an international setting, consider checking your milk (double- or triple-Ziploc-bagged) and ice packs in your checked baggage.

Keeping Your Milk Cold

Once you get through security, resist the urge to open the bag and look at your precious little milk bags in there. Keep the coldness inside. If you get horribly delayed, go find a bar and ask for ice. If you look new mom-ish enough, a bartender or waiter is likely take pity on you. If you have to change planes, you can (but usually don't have to, if it's not a long layover) fill your Ziploc bags with ice in the transfer airport, via another kind bartender. If you forget Ziploc bags, breastmilk storage bags make good substitutes for holding ice.

Once you are on the plane, if you are nervous about keeping the milk cold, you can ask the flight attendant if you can put the whole thing in the airplane fridge. Many will say no because they are not technically allowed to do it. You might get a kindhearted person who will bend the rules, but it's not really even necessary to do this on a direct flight, or even with a plane change. If you are super worried, they are likely to at least give you access to their ice for refills. Store your bag under the seat in front of you so it will be less jostled and you can keep an eye on it.

Getting Home

When you get to your destination, the frozen milk will probably be slushy or liquid around the edges. When I fly with milk and this happens, I just throw it back in the freezer and don't think about it again. Breastmilk is so stable, and it has so many white blood cells in it to kill bad stuff, that I just don't worry about it too much. Other moms have their own comfort levels, and their own tricks, like pouring off any liquid milk into "near-term" bottles to use within the next few days, and putting the fully frozen stuff into the freezer.

Some women ship milk home. I hated this idea until I met Robyn Roche-Paull, the badass mama who is a lactation consultant and a former Aviation Structural Mechanic in the U.S. Navy. More to the point, Robyn is the author of *Breastfeeding in Combat Boots*, a breastfeeding guide for active duty military women. Robyn says you can ship milk home with or without dry ice:

> Package your milk carefully to ensure that it gets to your caregiver, and ultimately to your baby, in perfect shape and ready to use. Frozen breastmilk packed properly will generally stay frozen long enough to withstand shipping up to 72 hours without the use of dry ice.
>
> Begin by putting four bags of frozen milk into a paper lunch bag, and then wrap with another lunch bag, forming a 'milk pack.' Once you have them all wrapped in the lunch bags, put a few of these milk packs in a gallon Ziploc bag, creating

packages of milk. Then either surround your block of dry ice with milk packs or, if you're not using dry ice, line the cooler (hard-sided is best) and layer the packages with newspaper.

Fill the remaining space with wadded-up newspaper. Pack the cooler in a shipping box, secure it well with packing tape, and label it 'fragile and perishable.'

Only DHL, FedEx, and UPS accept dry ice; they also ship internationally (there may be a hazardous materials fee added on). The U.S. Post Office does not accept dry ice. If you're shipping from abroad, you may also have to fill out customs paperwork and/or USDA or IRS paperwork.

Find more at www.breastfeedingincombatboots.com

Chapter 14: Traveling with Your Baby

You might have the option of bringing your baby with you on a short business trip, with a helpful grandparent, nanny, or spouse along for the journey. But should you? And how do you do it?

Should I Bring My Baby?

Bringing a baby on a business trip can be an alluring idea. You don't have to leave the baby behind, so there's less sadness and guilt. It might seem like less hassle because you can breastfeed instead of pumping and traveling home with milk. But it does have its own share of considerations.

Every business trip is different, but most are more hectic than a normal workday. You have people to impress, new locations to navigate, and a to-do list to hustle through. This is going to make breastfeeding your baby difficult, but with a really engaged caregiver/companion, liberal use of your cell phones, and friendly hosts, it might be doable.

One consideration on whether to bring your baby is how your colleagues will react and how much you care about that. If you plan on having your baby brought to you to feed, you might end up having to breastfeed your baby in front of these people, and they almost certainly will see you flustered and dealing with a crying or uncooperative infant.

Other considerations include how busy your schedule will be and whether your breaks will be predictable. If you are not in control of your schedule, or foresee very few breaks, you might end up not seeing much of your baby anyway while still having the stress of pumping and getting the milk to the baby's caregiver.

Olga, an academic, had to travel to a conference. She recounted, "I couldn't concentrate. I was running in and out of the room checking on him and breastfeeding."

If you are in the driver's seat on your schedule, you might find it relatively easy to plan breastfeeding meet-ups with your baby and her caregiver.

A final area to ponder is the potential upside of a business trip without your baby. Some women enjoy the alone time and use the opportunity to rest, network with colleagues, or binge-watch TV in their hotel rooms.

Making it Work

If you decide to bring your baby, get advance approval in writing (email is fine) from your manager and/or HR department.

Allies at your destination can help you find a place to breastfeed or pump (there may be times on this trip when it's not feasible to nurse your baby), and you'll probably want their support when you have your baby brought to you.

A facility with its own on-site daycare might allow your baby to hang out for the day, but make sure your baby is up to date on all vaccinations and check in advance in case there is paperwork required. Some locations might offer a vacant office or room for your baby and her caregiver.

If, instead, your caregiver will be offsite with the baby—at the hotel or strolling around a new city—plan to stay in close communication about feeding times. If it's not feasible for you or for the caregiver to reunite you and the baby for a feeding, be prepared to pump, and make sure the caregiver is equipped with a back-up feeding option (breastmilk or formula and a bottle).

Prepping Your Co-Workers

Mixing breastfeeding and work always results in conversations on the spectrum from productive to inappropriate with co-workers. To a certain extent, you can control when and how you have those conversations, but if you're traveling with your baby, it's in your best interest to address it proactively with any co-workers joining you on your trip and with anyone from your host organization who might be directly affected by your baby coming along.

Some people need to know because they'll be incredibly helpful if they are aware of what you are trying to accomplish. Others need to know because telling them will forestall them from making awkward comments in the moment. And then there's that special class of co-worker who tends to get outraged and cry "unfair!" at almost anything. This person might be annoyed that you're bringing your baby with you while his kids are back home in daycare, or she might not have kids and tends to think that any accommodation for a working parent is an unjust perk.

In all of these situations, being up front before your baby makes an appearance will help you avoid uncomfortable situations or confrontations. Tell your fellow travelers, as simply as possible, that your baby will be joining you on the trip and that you have cleared this with your manager and with HR. Don't go into deep detail on your daily schedule; just note that there will be times during the day when you'll need to feed your baby, and you will do your best to make this work with the demands of the trip. End by stating that you're hopeful that your co-worker(s) will be supportive.

If, in the moment, a co-worker (or anyone else, really) makes a negative comment or gives you a pointed look, try to focus on what you need to get done rather than on winning this particular fight. Responding in anger doesn't always make you look or feel good; getting the job done usually does. If you feel you have to respond because the comment is so egregious or it's a question that requires an answer, keep your tone and your answer neutral and brief. Remember that you got sign-off to do this. You don't have to remind people of that, because you might come off as defensive, but just knowing that it's true will give you confidence.

Nursing in Public

I could write a whole book about nursing in public, or NIP, as it's fantastically abbreviated. Everything about the debates on the topic makes me crazy: whether women should do it, whether they should have to use nursing covers to do it, and whether it's okay for strangers to take photos of them doing it and then using those photos to shame them on the internet. But if I get started, I'll never stop, so I'm moving on to practicalities.

Some women bring their babies with them on business trips simply so they can be together in the mornings and evenings; the baby stays with a caregiver during working hours, and the mother pumps as she would during normal work hours. Others have their babies with them for part or all of the workday, in a sling or stroller, with or without a caregiver on hand to help. This latter group will end up nursing their babies during the workday, and often not in complete privacy.

I'm not going to tell you what level of comfort you should have with NIP; in fact, no one should tell you that. It's a personal decision. Anyway, sometimes the baby takes charge: some older babies simply won't tolerate a cover over their heads, so their mothers, who do eventually have to go out in public with their babies, give up on trying to be ultra-discreet.

In thinking about NIP and work, I'm assuming you work somewhere other than some sort of midwives' cooperative, where you'd probably get high-fived for nursing out in the open. The more likely scenario is that you'll be nervous about everything from someone seeing your nipple to otherwise coming off as unprofessional. You might have to deal with looks (real or perceived) and comments, and your co-workers, clients, or hosts will see you as they've never seen you before. You might also be pleasantly surprised by how much (some) people like babies.

If you have time before this trip, I highly recommend breaking the seal now: get out in public with your baby and get comfortable with your version of NIP. The first time you nurse your baby in public is almost never graceful, but with practice, most women get really good at it. Wear layers and bring a blanket or hooter hider, if that's your thing, and practice nursing with and without it, in case your baby decides to call the shots. If your baby is a cover-hater, those layers can come in handy: pulling up the front of a cardigan can at least make you feel a little protected from view.

Once you're on the business trip, the most modest approach to nursing a baby requires finding private places to breastfeed, like vacant offices, mothers' lounges, storage closets, or a chair dragged into a restroom. Go back to Chapter 12 for a refresher on making allies to help you find private places, on calling ahead, and on making these places work for pumping, because most of those rules apply to nursing, too. In a pinch, facing a chair into the corner of a room might have to do.

Flying with Your Baby

Flying with a tiny baby is relatively easy, actually, because they sleep a lot and don't need any real toys or entertainment. Crawlers and toddlers are the ones who make air travel a living hell, which is a topic for another book entirely.

Before you leave, go to Target.com or Diapers.com and send diapers and wipes ahead to your hotel or host office.

Here's what you need for the plane:
- Two onesies that you wouldn't mind throwing away if they get poop all over them.
- Half a pack of wipes. Set aside a pack at home when it's half used up, to have a smaller item in your carry-on bag.
- If you use pacifiers, put one in every pocket of your pants.
- Snacks that are easy to open and eat.
- A blanket or swaddling wrap, if you swaddle your baby.
- An iPod or phone with podcasts or music or movies. Holding a baby for a whole flight can get very boring, and it's hard to read in that position.
- A bit of formula, or a bottle of breastmilk, for the caregiver.
- Dress the baby warmly (but if you use socks, know that you will never arrive at your destination with both of them).
- A sling or baby carrier.
- A stroller and car seat (especially if babywearing tires you out). Take these to the gate and gate check them.

When you board, look for kindly flight attendants. Some of them love to hold a little baby, which can be an essential break for you. Is someone flying with you? If not, don't drink much liquid; peeing is officially a luxury activity while you're on this airplane.

Nurse the baby for takeoff and landing. The swallowing helps their ears pop and cuts down on crying. Bring a nursing cover if you care about that kind of thing, and wait until the plane is speeding down the runway. If you start too early and there's a delay, the baby could finish nursing before takeoff. If your baby is fast asleep, just get your boob out and ready under the cover and don't force her to eat unless she wakes up and is uncomfortable. If takeoff and landing don't time right with her feeding schedule, you can just feed her a little and cut her off.

One final note: Do not expect to look good when you land.

Section 4: Problem Solving

Technically speaking, this whole book is about problem solving: solving the big question of bringing your baby's food source to work with you every day and all of the little problems that creates. But most of what we've covered so far is par for the course in working and breastfeeding (yes, even pumping on a public toilet counts as "par for the course"). What follows, in this final section, is a review of those things that can go really and truly wrong and how to address them.

Chapter 15: Supply and Supplementing

Supply stress happens to nearly every working, breastfeeding mother. It's just difficult for our bodies to react the same way to a pump as they do to a nursing baby, and it's worse for some women than it is for others. Add in work stress, forgetting to eat and drink, and not always getting in the pumping time we need, and it's easy to understand why so many working mothers experience stressful drops in supply or end up weaning altogether.

When supply issues hit and thoughts of supplementing crop up, you've arrived at the heart of many of the Mommy Wars debates around breastfeeding. I want to remind you that my goal in this book is not to advocate for any particular kind of infant feeding. I'm not pro-formula or pro-exclusive breastfeeding. I'm pro-whatever works for you, your life, and your goals.

The long story short is that you alone are in charge of this decision. You can ask friends and lactation professionals to support and encourage you, but in the end, your course is yours, and it might even change over time as your situation changes.

Do You Have a Supply Problem?

Before doing anything else, take the time to figure out if your supply is actually dipping or if your pump needs a tune-up or your expectations are off. Lactation experts say that the most common reason moms stop breastfeeding is perceived, rather than actual, insufficient milk supply. Often, making less milk than the baby is consuming is not a supply problem, but an over-feeding or under-pumping problem. How do you figure out if you have a real supply problem?

- Do some maintenance. Have a lactation professional or a store that sells or rents your brand of pump check your pump's motor. Make sure you have the right size flanges—you never want to see your nipples rubbing against the tube part of the flange. Replace the membranes. Replace the tubing or snip a small section off the ends for a better fit. Replace anything else that's replaceable.
- Ask other mothers what they're pumping. Sometimes just knowing what the range of "normal" looks like can help.
- Experiment with your baby's caregiver on giving slightly smaller bottles. See Chapter 4 for more detail on potential over-feeding.

Addressing Supply Issues

The standard breastfeeding books have lots of information on supply, so I will not duplicate what they offer, but a few pointers are necessary here because of the direct link between pumping at work and supply issues:

- Shop around for a lactation professional. Ask for her take on working and breastfeeding. If you're open to formula, ask her how she feels about that. If she doesn't get your situation, or seems to not respect your parenting decisions, maybe she's not the one for you.

- For a few days after you suspect a problem, pump every morning after the first morning feeding (like you did while first building your stash). You may only get an ounce or two, but you will be sending your body the message, at the beginning of every day, that it needs to make more milk.

- Extend the duration of each pumping session for a couple of days. Let the pump continue to run for five to ten minutes after milk stops coming out. It is not comfortable. It is not fun. But it tells your body that it needs to make more milk.

- As your milk starts to slow down, switch the pump back to the stimulation (fast) phase to try for another letdown.

- Increase the frequency of your pumping sessions, rather than the length.

- Power pump. This means pumping for short amounts of time over the course of the day, without washing the pump parts or necessarily putting away the milk (since it can sit at room temperature). For example, pump for five minutes every half hour over the course of several hours.

- Go to second base with yourself. Compress (squeeze and massage) your breasts while you pump. Especially look for little knots, which can release milk if you massage them while pumping. You can also lean forward and shake your breasts before you pump or run a comb lightly over them to release endorphins. These are actual techniques, by the way, not things I made up just to make you feel like a total weirdo.

- Try dietary changes. Some women swear by oatmeal, water, protein, or dark beer (hooray!).
- When you are with your baby, breastfeed as much as possible (unless you're an exclusive pumper, meaning someone who never nurses the baby, and only provides breastmilk by way of pumping).
- Try supplements (called galactogogues in lactation-speak). With my first baby, I took fenugreek. You have to take enough for your skin to smell like maple syrup (it's a lot). There are also fenugreek teas and lactation teas and cookies which often contain fenugreek. *Note: fenugreek is contraindicated for people with peanut allergies, blood sugar issues, and more. Before taking any supplements, check with a lactation professional or doctor.*
- Talk to your doctor about prescription medication to increase supply, but use caution. Reglan is not recommended for women with a history of depression, and can even lead to depressive symptoms in women with no prior history. Domperidone is not regularly available in the U.S. Both come with other cautions about their use.
- It's common to have a star boob and a poor performer. To a certain extent, it's normal. But if it's a major difference, you can try to give that little sad boob some TLC. Leave the pump running on that side longer. When you nurse your baby directly,

start him on that boob every time, to give it more demand. You could even sneak in an extra pumping session just on that side for a few days. Add all this up and you might see the little gal start to perk up a bit.

- DO NOT LOOK AT THE BOTTLES. Don't watch the milk come out, and don't watch the bottles to see how much they are filling up. Look at your phone, your laptop, a magazine, a picture of your baby—anything but the bottles.

Making Peace with Supplementing

If you really do have a supply problem, and the tactics above fail you, or if they work but you're making yourself long-term nuts and exhausted in the process, it might be time for you to consider supplementing with formula. Your baby is, obviously, super important. Also important? You, and your mental health. You are the very best-placed person to make informed decisions about how to feed your baby.

Many women I interviewed pointed to work as the reason for having to stop exclusively breastfeeding. It's that "exclusive" word I want to talk about first. Our generation of women tends to be so driven and goal-oriented that when we hear "breastfeed for a year," some of us automatically assume that means we have to *exclusively* breastfeed with no formula supplementation (but with solid foods starting at around six months).

That was certainly the case for me with my first baby. I viewed anything less than exclusive breastfeeding as a failure on my part. In my case, what this meant was that when my son was nine months old, I ran completely out of the physical and mental energy to continue to pump at work, on airplanes, and in random international locations. And I quit.

I didn't make it to the year that I had hoped for. The three months of formula before I switched him to cow's milk at a year felt like clear evidence of my failure. I shed a lot of tears, lost a lot of sleep, and struggled with a really ugly amount of anxiety.

You might worry that supplementing with formula is the beginning of the end of breastfeeding—that by supplementing regularly you are telling your body it doesn't need to figure out how to produce milk, and that this produces a vicious cycle of your body staying at its current production level, and you continuing to have to supplement.

But this so-called "vicious cycle" is not necessarily the end of breastfeeding, as long as you keep your eye on it. As many practical breastfeeding educators note, breastfeeding doesn't have to be all or nothing.

The reality of working and breastfeeding often means an eventual drop in supply below what your baby demands—sometimes temporary, sometimes permanent. So while the exclusive breastfeeding advocates might scare you away from what I am about to tell you, I will say that this is an idea that revolutionized my life: done right, supplementing with formula can be a powerful tool to help you *keep* breastfeeding.

With my second child, I took an entirely different approach from what I did with my first. Knowing that my job would continue to be stressful, that I would continue to travel every single month, and that the whole thing would be exhausting, I began to think of formula as a potential ally in my success rather than the proof of my failure.

If I could use formula as supplementation when my body wasn't making enough milk, I knew I could take a lot of the anxiety and pressure off, and get some balance back in my life.

Before my daughter was born, I asked three girlfriends—all mothers—to keep me accountable to not going back to my most anxious self. I told them that when my daughter was three months old, I wanted a phone call or visit from each of them, asking me to confirm that I had given her an ounce of formula—one single ounce. (As noted in Chapter 4, there are some drawbacks to introducing formula this early on; I made a personal decision to do this, based on my own experiences with postpartum anxiety related to breastfeeding.)

I made these friends promise that if I hadn't done it, they were to come to my house and literally smack me. In the face. (Everyone needs friends who will promise to slug them in a dire situation.)

Knowing I had this promise (and the potential of being hit) out in the world, I asked my husband to try a bit of formula on my daughter when she was six weeks old just to make sure she could tolerate it. Then we put the formula away and didn't take it out again for months—so long, in fact, that when we did, it had expired and we had to chuck it and buy a new can.

I eventually turned to more consistent supplementing with formula when my daughter was a bit older and I just could not keep up after a long workday. I was actually pumping about the same amount as her daytime feedings, but when it came to evenings, my girl was still hungry, and no amount of cluster feeding seemed to be keeping her satisfied. I also knew that if we dipped into the freezer stash every night for the two to four ounces she seemed to need, we'd be dry pretty soon.

So I started to see formula as my friend. It was helping my daughter get what she needed, when she needed it, and enabling me to keep pumping at work without feeling like a failure.

This formula thing also had some unexpected benefits:

- I knew my daughter tolerated formula, so when I amused myself by lying in bed freaking out over what would happen to my kids if I were hit by a car or something, what my baby would eat was not part of the doom scenario.
- I stopped stressing about business trips. If the milk in the freezer ran out, my husband would use formula.
- I had not a glimmer of the postpartum anxiety I went through the first time. Maybe this was just because I felt more in control.
- I became less protective of my stash. When my neighbor had a baby and had to go back to the hospital a few days later, I gave her several bags of frozen breastmilk to last until she got back home. When my co-worker's stash ran low, I gave her 60 ounces with a smile. I donated 180 ounces to my milk bank. And I loved all of it.

Supply Issues and Supplementing

If you go back to work and never experience a significant supply issue, I'm thrilled for you. But if you're working, chances are you'll have some supply issues, like these women:

Amie, a consultant: "Despite my commitment, eventually my body just wasn't making enough milk to keep up."

Jessica, a lawyer: "If I stressed about supplementing as a working parent, I probably would get so stressed that I might stop pumping. I admit I would rather she be 100% breastfed, but you do what you can when you're working."

Elise, a teacher: "I had unrealistic expectations, and should have been much gentler on myself."

Carla, an advertising professional: "I had to start supplementing at six months and the supplementing naturally got higher and higher until I quit pumping altogether at ten months. But I was able to continue nursing mornings and evenings until thirteen months!"

Claire, a lawyer: "Yeah, I supplemented. That doesn't mean I didn't breastfeed my child. Ask my husband: my boobs were off-limits and working pretty hard for those seven months."

These stories helped me realize that maybe formula is not the enemy. My biggest issue with modern motherhood debates is that they are presented as so black-and-white. Co-sleep or sleep train. Schedule or demand feed. Breastfeed or don't. The camps are formed and the enemies are clear. But we are complex individuals. Every circumstance is different, and differing choices are valid.

Providing some breastmilk should be seen as a triumph. So should investing in a healthy *you*, because you matter to your baby, and you matter, period. If supplementing—whether for a few days or on an ongoing basis—allows you to continue to provide some breastmilk or restores you to a place of sanity, then formula might be your friend.

Take note that consistently supplementing with formula (rather than occasionally) tells your supply to stay where it is, and this decision will probably cause you to have to supplement for the duration of breastfeeding. But you know what that looks like to me? That looks like problem solving. It looks like success.

Staying Exclusive

There are many women who want to avoid formula as long as their babies are healthy, hydrated, and growing. It should go without saying (but I'm saying it) that these women's experiences and goals are valid and should be supported. A good number of working women successfully stick with exclusive breastfeeding, and find it hugely gratifying.

Jenny, a nurse: "I was very proud of myself and my body."

Heather, a marketing manager: "Sticking with it finally resulted in something clicking. One day I realized, I can do this! Things fell into place and I'm thankful I gutted it out."

For women who want to feed their babies breastmilk only, the supply-increasing tactics above are important. Many lactation professionals also recommend safe co-sleeping as a way to breastfeed through the night (please talk to your lactation professional and/or pediatrician to make sure you're doing this right). If your baby is sleeping through the night and upping your supply is of utmost importance to you, you can set an alarm and get up to pump instead.

If your personal commitment to exclusive breastfeeding outweighs all other considerations and your job just doesn't allow for it, you can also make changes at your workplace. Ask for a flexible schedule, get permission to have your baby brought to you to be fed, work from home, or look for a new job altogether.

Chapter 16: Weaning

Some working women find they can breastfeed for as long as they like, taking their cues from their babies as to when it's time to wean. Others have the decision made for them when work pressures make it impossible to pump (it is worth noting again that many working mothers end up continuing to breastfeed morning and evening with no pumping at work; this all depends on your supply). Many women, however, find that weaning becomes a proactive decision, because they've reached their own personal milestone or simply know it's time to stop.

> Samantha describes her decision to wean this way: "I knew when I had pushed myself as far as I could go, and I weighed my options with the big picture of my own emotional and physical health in mind."

> Maria told me, when I asked her how she solved her really terrible insomnia brought on by breastfeeding hormones (this happens to a few unfortunate women), "I switched to formula. Worked like a charm."

When to Do It

Weaning can be confusing and is one of those mixed-emotion territories. For me, with both of my kids, I felt really emotional and conflicted leading up to the actual last feeding. I mourned—in advance—the loss of this thing that only I could give my baby. I finally put down my iPhone during those early morning feedings, remembering to snuggle and breathe in all that baby goodness instead of checking my email while the baby ate.

I dreaded the loss of my temporary boob job and the return to my lifetime of flat-chestedness. (I have never fully gotten over the anthem of my eighth grade year, chanted at me by the boys in my class: "Roses are red/Violets are black/Why is your chest/As flat as your back?") I fretted over my decision, whether it would hurt my baby, whether I'd regret it, and whether I should just go another day, another week, another month.

With both kids, my husband saw my mental and physical state and eventually told me it was a good time to stop, and I was grateful to outsource the decision. I know some women who have had to deal with the opposite—a spouse who applies pressure to keep going—and I would like to give those spouses a swift kick in the ass.

Miraculously, after weaning both times, I was happy. I wasn't the only person who had to get up first in the morning. I could plan to do something—see a friend, work late, exercise (just kidding!)—without doing the mental aerobics of "Is there enough milk thawed at home, do I need to bring my pump, where will I pump," and on and on and on.

Even more rewarding to me was the fact that I could focus on playing with my child rather than doing all the feeding. I remember watching my husband in the mornings with our kids (once he eventually got out of bed—love you, honey!). He got to just *play* with them. Meanwhile, I had spent the first twenty minutes of the day nursing, so the rest of my morning was a frenzy of brushing teeth, eating, chugging coffee, making lunches, and getting out the door. With both kids, it wasn't until after I completely stopped breastfeeding that I realized that I had traded in one kind of bond—nursing—to create space for new ways of connecting with my baby.

Everyone is different. You might have no angst at all about weaning, which does not make you a heartless monster. You might agonize over it and go for a year, or two, or more, which does not make you creepy. But if you are not comfortable waiting for your baby to lead the way and a dwindling milk supply doesn't make the decision for you, you will probably have to actively wean your baby at some point. So the answer to "When do I wean?" is both simple and complex. In short: When breastfeeding is no longer mutually beneficial for mom and baby.

The long answer: every situation is different, and breastfeeding relationships often change rapidly and unexpectedly. One week you might be sure you'll never make it, and you'll hang in a bit longer and find yourself in a decent groove again. Or you might fight an uphill battle the whole way and collapse across whatever finish line you happen to be at when you run out of gas. You might find yourself with a two-year-old and think, "Wow! That wasn't so bad!" You might think your kid is self-weaning, and then a week later he's back with a vengeance. There truly is no telling.

It's not for a single other person to decide. It's your body, your milk, your baby, your hormones, your *self* hooked up to a machine at work. Your baby is important, of course, but you get to think of yourself in this process, too. If breastfeeding is causing you terrible anxiety, ruining your performance at work, hurting your relationship with your kids or your spouse—all of these are valid factors. You are more than the milk you make, and you are in charge of your body.

And, after all, we all wean eventually, be it at five days or five years. It's something each of us will go through, and I am a firm believer that it has to be on your timetable, for your reasons.

How to Do It

Weaning can be abrupt or gradual. There is no one way to do it, and I'm not going to cover every weaning strategy in the world. You will find your own way with the help of mom friends, Facebook support groups (just make sure they're not full of judgy moms, like the ones who kicked me out of their group for deciding to wean my daughter at thirteen months instead of their preferred two years), and lactation professionals (you can even find some on Twitter who will answer questions for you—search for hashtags like #bfing or #bfcafe).

At its core, mother-led weaning, rather than letting the baby set the pace over months or years, means finding ways to drop feedings over time to lessen your supply and transition your baby over to other forms of liquid nourishment (formula or donor milk for under-ones, cow's milk, goat's milk, almond milk, or even just water with plenty of other sources of calcium and protein and fat for toddlers).

I've found that having a plan for dropping feedings, and giving myself time—weeks rather than days—has helped a lot with minimizing pain, engorgement, and plugged ducts. (Plugged ducts? Sound familiar? In fact, many of the early stuff that happens when your milk comes in can happen again as you intentionally wean. Engorged breasts, leaking, spraying, plugged ducts—even mastitis can rear its ugly head as your body adjusts once again to changing circumstances.)

Keep in mind, too, that introducing solid foods (including purees, because "solid" just means "not milk") is part of weaning, too. Solids for babies under a year are for experimentation, learning how to eat, getting some extra nutrition, and testing for food sensitivities, and most of your baby's nutrition should still come from what she drinks from breast or bottle. But once your baby starts to eat "real food," she has begun to wean.

Dropping Feedings

When I say "dropping" feedings in the context of weaning, I don't mean skipping that feeding for your baby. When the baby is hungry, the baby gets to eat. When your *baby* drops a feeding, that means she takes one less feeding in a 24-hour-period. A newborn might eat twelve times a in a day, and a six-month-old baby five to eight times. You can work with your spouse and your caregiver to understand when the baby really is hungry so no one is pushing milk on her when she doesn't truly want it. It's often easier to tell that your baby wants to drop a feeding when you're away at work, because the baby might nurse with you just to enjoy the snuggle, but might, when you're gone, take a very short feeding or push the bottle away when offered it. If this happens consistently, maybe baby is ready to shift the schedule.

What we're talking about with weaning is *you* dropping the number of times your body makes feedings in a single day; in other words, you deciding to decrease the number of times you ask your body to produce milk. Your baby's number of feedings won't necessarily change, but you'll be making the gradual transition to offering the breast (or pumping milk while at work) less and less.

Let's look at a step-by-step process to do this over the course of a few weeks. Remember, please, that I am not a lactation professional, just a fellow traveler on this weird journey:

First, think about the number of feedings your baby is taking per day. Is your baby a year old or older and doing three liquid feeds (breast or bottle) per day? Is she three months old and feeding eight to ten times a day, including at night? For our purposes, we're going to use three scenarios: (a) a baby taking four or more feedings a day, (b) a baby taking three feedings a day, and (c) a different approach: dropping feedings only as your baby drops them.

Weaning

Scenario A: Baby takes four or more daily milk feedings

Example: a six month old, just starting to eat purees, who is nursing or taking a bottle six times a day, including one nighttime feeding.

Look at those feedings and decide which is best for you to stop breastfeeding or pumping for. The milk your baby gets at this feeding will start to come from formula or your breastmilk stash. You might choose to stop breastfeeding for the middle-of-night feeding and "let" your spouse do that one. How lovely for him or her, getting to enjoy the sweet midnight bonding sessions with the baby!

If you choose this midnight feeding to drop, keep a hand pump set up next to your bed. I recommend a hand pump, rather than the full electric thing, because I find a hand pump, or hand expressing, gives you much more control over taking out just enough milk to get comfortable. With an electric pump, there's too much risk of it causing a big letdown and continuing the demand cycle for more milk. You might wake up feeling very full, and will need to "pump to comfort" and go back to sleep (cap the bottle and leave the milk out until morning–remember how stable breastmilk is!–or you can keep a cooler and ice packs next to your bed). Do *not* do a full pumping session, which would tell your body to keep making lots of nighttime milk. Just pump to take the edge off.

You might instead choose to drop a daytime pumping session while you're at work. Let's say you're pumping three times a day at work. Drop it to two, and hand pump or hand express if you get too full. Remember, the number of feedings your baby gets doesn't change; only the number of times you are demanding milk from your body.

Once you've completed this drop, wait a while. Let yourself get to a new steady state of Baby's Feedings Minus One. Give it a week or so to let your supply adjust.

After that "new normal" week, it's time to drop again. Let's say you now breastfeed or pump five times a day, while the baby is eating six times a day.

Look at these five feedings and figure out which one you want to drop next. Night time? Workday? Morning so you can sleep in? You'll know the drill better now.

Repeat until you are down to breastfeeding or pumping three times a day. Now you're ready to move to Scenario B.

Scenario B: Baby takes three daily milk feedings

This is most likely a baby at or above the one-year mark, doing bottle or breast feedings morning, lunchtime, and before bed. (If your one-year-old feeds more frequently than this, don't stress: that's normal, too!)

If your baby is down to three feedings total, you are probably only pumping once during the workday. The easiest thing for you to do is drop that single pumping session at work. Continue to bring a hand pump to work with you in case you get engorged, and wear breast pads and keep a back-up stash nearby. On weekends (or whenever you're off

Weaning

work), you can either give a bottle at lunchtime, or go back to nursing at lunchtime.

In this scenario, many women will still make enough milk to continue morning and evening feedings indefinitely, but if you find your supply dropping for those two feedings, as evidenced by a much hungrier baby after you breastfeed, your supply might be diminishing, thereby speeding up the weaning process for you.

If you don't want that weaning process to speed up because you enjoy those morning and evening feedings, consider going back to pumping once during the workday in order to maintain enough supply to do the morning and evening feeds.

After you drop from three feedings to two, give yourself another week for your body to adjust. You'll know you're there when you no longer have to pump to take the edge off in the middle of the workday.

Now here's where it gets tricky. If you're nursing (or pumping, for you exclusive pumpers) mornings and evenings, you are probably in a decent equilibrium. You wake up full but not engorged, and you are full again by evening, but your body has adjusted. But how do you go from twice a day to once?

As always, this is up to you, but most people I've talked to—including lactation professionals—recommend dropping the morning feeding first. It's partly the niceness of evening snuggles and setting the baby up for a good bedtime. It's also partly getting to sleep in some mornings. And, in the morning, your baby is more likely to be alert and ready to party, so you (or your spouse) can get her up, play with her, and distract her from the fact that she's not snuggled up and breastfeeding.

The most important thing in this scenario is to break your normal morning nursing routine. For example, if you usually bring your baby into bed and nurse her there, do not bring her to bed and give her a bottle. For the first few days, if it's possible, have someone else get up with the baby (woo hoooooo!).

This person should get the baby and go into another room and play for a bit. He or she should not give the bottle immediately, as part of this process is teaching the baby she doesn't need to eat the very instant she wakes up. This is a new routine. Play, walk around, whatever, and *then* sit down to breakfast with baby, offering a sippy cup or bottle of milk or formula, or even just food and water at that time.

You, back in bed, might need to do a little hand pumping or hand expressing to relieve the pressure. As always, when you drop this feeding, give your body about a week to adjust. Especially with this drop, you need to pay attention to engorgement, plugged ducts, and the potential for mastitis. (For more on mastitis, see Chapter 17 and the resources listed in Chapter 19.)

Once you are down to only one breastfeeding or pumping session per day, be it morning or night, it's time to take a deep breath and drop that final one. For some women, one "demand" a day might not be enough to sustain your supply anyway, so your body might solve this problem for you. For others, you will still have to actively drop this one.

Decide what your last breastfeeding session will be with this baby, ever, and allow yourself a good cry or celebration, or both.

The next couple of days, be prepared to hand-express or lightly use a hand pump, removing just enough milk to feel comfortable. Watch your body carefully for the coming week, and don't be surprised if you have some leaking for weeks (sometimes months) to come.

Scenario C: Dropping feedings as your baby drops them

When my daughter was nine months old, she was on a pretty predictable eating schedule: 7 a.m., 11 a.m., 1 p.m., 3 p.m., and 7 p.m., give or take half an hour either side of each time. (She had finally stopped waking at 4 a.m. for a snack.)

At this point, I was pumping three times during my workday. So, to start the weaning process, I could have just pumped at 10 a.m. and 3 p.m., dropping one pumping session. But around this time, my daughter started to freak out when the nanny tried to feed her at 11 a.m., which was a sign that the baby was trying to drop a feeding herself.

We experimented with our caregiver moving the 11 a.m. feeding to noon or 1 p.m., and doing another feeding at 3 or 4 p.m. This worked, so my daughter was now down to four feedings total every day. So I followed her: I went down to pumping twice in the workday. In other words, she dropped a feeding so I dropped a pumping session along with her. We were even again.

You can push ahead of your baby by dropping pumping sessions faster than she drops feedings, or you can follow along and drop sessions as the baby drops her own feedings. In the former case, you set the tempo. In the latter case, the baby does—just know that committing to the baby-led route could mean breastfeeding for a year or two, or more. The good news, in both directions, is that you can reevaluate and change over time. You can do mother-led, long-term weaning, and then change your mind and let the baby take charge. You might think you're going to let your baby lead, but later make the decision that you're going to step in and wean. You're the boss.

Drying Up Supply

There are some things you can do proactively to help you dry up your milk supply (it follows that if you're trying to maintain or increase supply, it's best avoid these things). These include:

- Putting fresh cabbage leaves on your breasts to ease engorgement (roll them with a rolling pin or wine bottle first, then place one inside each bra cup until it is wilted).
- Taking a daily, safe dose of Sudafed or similar drug with pseudoephedrine (after talking with your doctor). This drug is known to adversely affect milk supply.
- Eating and drinking lots of peppermint and sage (in teas, essential oils, and foods).

Oh, the Guilt

After all that effort to breastfeed your baby, weaning can bring on feelings of guilt and remorse for some women. This is normal, but only you can decide what to do with those feelings: keep breastfeeding or stay the weaning course. If it helps, I have found some techniques that have helped me and my working mother friends with weaning guilt.

First, ask yourself how long you were breastfed. Chances are, you don't know the answer, or didn't until very recently, when you got curious and asked your mom. In fact, this might be the most boring piece of information about your entire childhood. That doesn't mean that breastfeeding isn't great and important. But somehow, realizing that I didn't give any thought to my own breastfeeding duration as a baby gave me some peace.

Second, make an effort to notice all the things you do with and for your baby that are not related to breastfeeding. Many women fear that weaning will somehow hurt their bond with their babies, so it's important to get some perspective on the many ways that bond is formed and maintained. Every tickle, every smile, every time you soothe or kiss or bathe that baby, make yourself notice these things and do not discount them just because they are something other than breastfeeding.

Weaning isn't hard for everyone, but if it happens before you want it to, it can bring on a lot of guilt and feelings of failure.

I'm not going to pretend that I can eliminate your Mom Guilt (or mine) as it relates to breastfeeding or anything else. But in writing this book, I did some reading about the difference between guilt and shame, and it's an important distinction. Guilt is a response to what you think you've done wrong. Shame is feeling that who you *are* is wrong.

Guilt says, "I had a hard time balancing breastfeeding and work, and I feel bad about it." Shame says, "I'm not a good mother because I failed at this." We are (usually) the only ones who can breastfeed our babies, so when it doesn't go well, we might think that we are not good enough for them. Or, maybe, just not good enough, period.

Guilt sucks, but it's got nothing on shame. Shame finds the bottommost part of your soul and takes up residence there. It colors how you look at everything and it sticks around for a long time. I want to leave you with a reminder that you have nothing to be ashamed of, no matter how breastfeeding turns out for you.

You are not a failure.

Your worth as a mother is not measured in ounces.

Say it out loud. Write it on the inside of your pump bag. You're a great mom doing a hard job, and I hope you're really proud of yourself.

Chapter 17: Surviving Disaster Days

All the preparation in the world will not prevent you from having a disastrous day. Your new-parent exhaustion will inevitably make you forget something, spill something, or screw something up. A sense of humor and a realization that this, too, shall pass are your most important tools in any of the stressful situations below. But I wouldn't be doing my job if I didn't give you some survival strategies, too—straight from the working mothers who have gone before you.

So without further ado, I bring you what to do if . . .

You Notice Your Milk Smells Funny

Some women go back to work only to find out (or hear from a caregiver) that the milk has "gone bad," "smells funny," or tastes "metallic" or "soapy." This often results in a lot of milk being thrown away. Before you dump the stuff (or let someone else do the same), consider this: that smell can sometimes be attributed to an enzyme called lipase that is present at higher levels in some women's breastmilk.

Lipase breaks down milk fats, and fat is part of what helps breastmilk taste good. Over time, as milk sits in the fridge or freezer, that lipase continues to work at breaking down those fats. And if you produce a lot of it, then there's more lipase to get the job done. Result? That soapy- or metallic-tasting milk.

Some babies of higher-lipase moms (mine included) don't seem to mind this different smell and taste at all, and it's perfectly safe for the baby. Others might refuse the milk, which is why it's so important to do some dry runs ahead of time. The last thing you need is this kind of stress on your first day back at work.

If you think you might have a lipase issue and you really want to be sure, take some of your milk and see a lactation professional or La Leche League group to find out for sure. You could also just try the tactics below and see what works.

If you determine that lipase is the culprit and your baby is taking the milk without complaint, carry on, and educate all caregivers about the smell so you don't have any unexpected dumpings. If your baby isn't happy about it, you can experiment with various storage methods. If milk that has been frozen is the issue, try using the day-to-day pumping method (pump Monday for Tuesday's bottle) to see if refrigerated milk fares better, or try freezing immediately after pumping to see if that helps. With a bit of trial-and-error, you might be able to determine how long it takes your milk to start getting that strange flavor.

You can also scald the milk briefly *before* refrigerating or freezing it. Scalding means heating the milk until just the edges of the milk begin to bubble, then immediately taking it off the heat to cool.

Scalding in a pot, which is what a lot of women do at home, will be difficult in some work situations. An alternative is to bring a bottle warmer to work and keep it in the lactation room or at your desk. This is not the most straightforward of processes. You will have to experiment with how much water to put into the warmer, as it can require more than you would need just to warm a baby bottle. Ideally, you'd also purchase a digital thermometer and put it into the breastmilk while it heats. Heat the milk until it reaches between 160 and 180 degrees Fahrenheit (opinions on temperature seem to vary, and women seem to have success at both ends of the range). Let the milk stay at that temperature for 30-60 seconds, then pull the milk out of the warmer and chill and store it. A final note: If you worry about the health impacts of heating and reheating plastic bottles to this temperature, use glass bottles. If you do use glass, move the milk to something plastic (a bottle or a breastmilk bag) to cool it.

For some women, scalding seems to take care of the smell and taste issues. While scalding does diminish some of the nutritional qualities of your breastmilk, the milk is still great for your baby. You could also try mixing breastmilk with formula, or scalded breastmilk with non-scalded breastmilk, to dilute the taste.

If you have exhausted every lipase remedy and nothing is working, all might not be lost. You could continue to pump to maintain supply, especially if you have a younger baby, and continue to attempt to offer a bottle on a regular basis. The issue might not be the taste, after all; it could be the temperature or the type of bottle (try a sippy cup for an older baby) or the way the baby is being held or many other things. If you feel determined to stick it out, giving it some time might be the right option for you.

If none of this works, and your baby hates the taste of your milk, well honey, you might be at the end of your pumping road (and if you are, you can still donate that frozen milk to a milk bank!). You can still breastfeed when you are with your baby, so the milk is fresh. Remember that breastfeeding does not have to be all or nothing.

You Leave a Bottle of Breastmilk Out All Day

This, my friend, happens to everyone. You'll do it, your spouse will do it, and your caregiver will do it. Breastmilk is oh-so-stable, because it has all that good stuff in it, and it can withstand being at room temperature for six or even eight hours. When this happens, get that bottle into the fridge, or into your baby, and move on with your day. If it's been out too long, close your eyes, say "renewable resource!" out loud, and dump it.

You Forget a Pump Part

You absolutely will forget some essential part of your pumping setup at some point. Count on it. To minimize this risk, add calendar reminders for morning and end of day, every day, to make sure you are hauling the parts you need. Keep dual sets of parts at home and at the office. Make sure your pump has a battery pack and that this pack stays with it at all times. Keep a hand pump at your desk as a back-up.

Bottles are the best thing to forget because there are real options that will allow you to still use your pump. You can steam-sterilize cups or glasses in the microwave by putting an ounce of water into the cup, covering it with plastic wrap or a saucer, and microwaving it for two minutes. You can attach milk storage bags or clean Ziploc bags to the pump connectors, either with the sticky strips some bags come with or with tape or rubber bands. (Note: this won't work for all pumps, because some pumps require a tight seal on the bottle in order to work.)

Leslie, a psychologist in an office within an OB/GYN department, forgot her bottles and used those sterile urine cups that pregnant moms are asked to pee in.

If you forget one flange, connector, or tube, you can still pump, albeit one boob at a time. Just remember to plug up the hole on the pump for the other side so you get normal suction.

If you forget both of any given part or lose your power source altogether, this is the same thing as forgetting your whole pump. This goes for tubes, connectors, flanges, and membranes. If this happens, short of having every Babies 'R' Us and Target in town mapped out for emergency purchases (this is actually a really good idea), there are a few tricks to help you get through the day:

- Keep a hand pump at your desk and in your car.
- Learn how to hand express, so you can avoid getting engorged. Most nursing books cover this. Your supply will not dry up in a

day of manually expressing, and you can even capture some milk in a sterilized cup.
- Get ready to have really incredible knockers for the day.

You Worry That Your Pump Is Not Working

You will absolutely have a workday in which your supply just seems off, and you will most likely panic about it. Give it a day or two, and try to relax in the meantime. But if you see a persistent problem, or if you suspect that your pump is not working properly, there are a few things to address that might do the trick:

- Check your power source. If you're using batteries, replace them on both sides of the battery pack. In fact, if you use batteries, try an outlet to see if that makes a difference.
- Make sure those membranes are in good working order. Or just replace them; sometimes that will do the trick.
- Get new tubing or cut off the ends of your existing tubes—assuming you have the kind that don't have that little plastic doohickey inside of them. This might help the tubes fit on the pump more snugly.
- Watch your nipples inside the flanges as you're pumping. Your nipples change size over time (I know: yuck), and if yours are rubbing against the inside of the tube part of the flange, it's time for a larger size flange.

If all of this fails and you still think it's your pump, take it to a lactation professional or a store that sells or rents pumps and ask them to test it.

You Spill or Leak Milk on Your Clothes

The best measures in this case are preventative: Bring an extra change of clothes to keep in your car or at your desk or a cardigan to cover shirt wetness. Patterned clothes can hide milk stains better than plain fabrics. But if you end up forgetting your preventative measures, you can at least try to clean up the damage a little bit.

> Sara, a corporate retail manager, was so tired one day that she forgot to attach bags or bottles to her pump. It took her a few minutes to realize she was pumping milk all over her pants.

While the milk is still wet, put a paper towel inside the garment (next to your skin), and another one on the outside, and press. This will help pull the liquid out from both sides, rather than just pressing on it from the outside. Keep an eye on it while it dries, especially for dark fabrics. It can leave a white ring around the outside of the spot, which you'll want to spot-treat with water.

You Forget Breast Pads

Toilet paper makes an okay nursing pad for your bra when you have forgotten your breast pads at home. Better? A maxi pad or panty liner cut in half; it even has adhesive! Or cut circles out of that unused diaper that always seems to be at the bottom of your purse.

You Get Engorged/Plugged Ducts/Mastitis

Engorgement is the bane of working mothers. It is going to happen because your boss or a client needs you, or you forget your pump at home, or you're traveling, or you just run out of time in the day. Breast pads are your friend for this and similar scenarios. Keep an eye on lower-cut tops, which can go from fine to risqué in an engorgement situation. If you get seriously overfilled and in pain and don't have the option of pumping, get to a bathroom and hand express until at least some of the pressure is taken off. You can do this into a spare breast pad, a sink, a toilet, a trash can, a breastmilk storage bag, a coffee cup (steam-sterilized in the microwave if you plan on saving the milk), or even your hand.

Plugged milk ducts can happen any time milk is trapped in your breast, like from an underwire or too-tight bra, sleeping on your chest, or nursing in one position only.

Plugged ducts are the close cousin of engorgement, although they can even happen when you have not been engorged. If you notice small hard spots in your breasts, don't panic. They do not necessarily mean that you are moments away from mastitis—or, as I freaked out over the first time, that you have breast cancer (I didn't).

Try to massage them, making small circles with good pressure, while pumping (and, at home, while nursing—your baby can be more efficient at clearing these up). When nursing your baby directly, try out different positions and holds—sometimes the baby latching in a different position, like with his chin pointing toward the clog, can draw milk from a different part of the breast.

If you have an electric toothbrush, you can use it on the outside of your breast, near the clog, to help break it up. Warm water may also help: fill a basin and dangle your breasts over it while massaging them, or stand in the shower and allow the spray to hit your back and roll down your chest. You can also do warm, wet washcloths (throw them in the microwave for thirty seconds and check their temperature so you don't burn your skin).

It might take a day or two, but keeping at this consistently can help. If you find this happening frequently, ask your doctor or lactation professional about solutions, including lecithin, a natural supplement that is safe for baby and helps prevent those little plugs.

Don't freak unless they become really painful and/or warm or if you get a fever. Those symptoms point toward mastitis, which requires a visit to your doctor to avoid more serious issues like an abscess. For most women, mastitis is overcome-able with antibiotics and the plugged duct tactics described here. Fever, warmth, pain, and redness usually need to be present for 24 hours before antibiotics are given.

You See Moisture in Your Pump Tubes

This happens a lot to working mothers, whose pump parts often don't have time to dry between sessions. You want to get on top of this to avoid mold or mildew growing inside your tubing, which will require you to replace them immediately. Whenever you see water or any moisture, do as follows:

Finish pumping but don't turn off the pump. Unplug the tubes from the connectors and leave them plugged into the pump. Let the pump run for a few minutes. Dry as a bone! If you feel the need to clean the tubes, you can wash with soapy water, rinse, and do this "run the pump to dry" trick again. You can also drip rubbing alcohol into the tubes, let them sit for a minute or two, and then swing the tubes around your head, lasso style (don't hit anyone!). If your pump is closed-system, note that you should never have to wash the tubing.

Your Baby Won't Take a Bottle

This is a particularly stressful situation for a working mother. You're at work with your baby's food source, and she's somewhere else, refusing the milk you are working so hard to produce. Some women have work situations that allow them to go to their babies, or have them brought to the workplace, for feedings. This doesn't work for many working women, however, so a talk with your pediatrician or lactation professional is probably in order.

Refer back to Chapter 4, where we talked about introducing a bottle to the baby. With patience and experimentation, almost every baby can be convinced to take a bottle—or maybe a sippy cup, which can work even for very young babies.

Experiment with the variables you have in front of you. Play with temperature (some babies want it warmer or colder). Play with the nipple size/shape/texture. Make bottlefeeding similar to the breastfeeding experience, or make it 100% unlike it. Offer the bottle while the baby is drowsy (and thus less opinionated, possibly). Have the caregiver hold something that smells like you.

You can also consider "reverse cycling," which accomplishes the basic goal of getting your baby enough milk. In short, you work toward your baby nursing frequently at night, and eating less during the day. This situation usually involves some kind of (Safe! Talk to your pediatrician!) co-sleeping arrangement, but the mother is on call all night long, so I never considered this a viable option for my sanity. But then again, some women find safe co-sleeping to give them *more* sleep, not less.

> Ann recalled, "My baby didn't want to take a bottle at all when I went back to work . . . even now, she prefers the breast, so at night it is 'boob o'clock' at my house. Babies might not eat much during the day, but they will make up for it at night and your body will adjust. The guilt, though, when your child hates a bottle at first, can be a lot for a working parent."

In the meantime, while you figure out whatever works for you, use small amounts of breastmilk at a time so your caregiver is not wasting anything.

Your Caregiver Gives the Baby a Bottle Just Before You Get Home

This is a classic working mother's frustration. You time your pumping sessions perfectly at work, then rush home, looking forward to giving up the pump until tomorrow and actually getting to nurse your baby. You walk in the door and the caregiver smiles and says, "Just finished a bottle!"

Managing this scenario requires early and frequent education of the caregiver, steady communication, and some grace and forgiveness on your part. Talk with the provider to make sure that they understand that nursing is a priority for you at the end of the day. Make sure they feel empowered to give a bottle if the baby is truly hungry and cannot wait, but stress that you'd like to try to make this work as often as possible. Arm them with tricks like giving the baby just an ounce from the bottle to take the edge off until you arrive. If possible, text or call just before you leave work so they have a heads-up about when you might arrive.

On those days when this happens (it will), take a deep breath and smile and know these people are doing the best they can. Many babies will nurse a little anyway just because they love their mamas. And bring that pump home daily, just in case!

You Want a Glass of Wine

My son, seeing me with an opaque drinking cup, once asked me, "Mama, is that wine or coffee?" For him, those are the only two things mom might be drinking. Go on, judge.

While pregnant, I indulged in a glass of wine here and there with the support of my OB/GYN. But when my son finally arrived, I was totally confused about breastmilk and drinking. While any new mother might wrestle with this decision, it actually can become a business issue when drinks after work and on business trips come into play.

No one can make this decision for you. What I can promise you is that if you do decide to drink a bit while breastfeeding, you will get judged—just not necessarily to your face. Might as well know that up front so you're prepared for it.

The American Academy of Pediatrics recommends that breastfeeding mothers avoid all alcohol. Here's my layperson's take on this issue: much of the available research seems to say that a drink or two will not hurt your baby (unless you give the drink *to* the baby, which you shall not do under any circumstances). For those who believe this and feel comfortable with it, there is a spectrum of how you might approach having a glass of wine or a beer or two.

Those who are terrified of the idea of mixing drinking and breastfeeding, but still want to imbibe, tend to "pump and dump"—that is, drink and then completely empty the breasts of milk and throw that milk away. This is a drastic move, and there are very limited situations in which it actually makes sense.

The way alcohol and breastmilk work together doesn't actually require you to pump and dump in most situations. Alcohol is metabolized in breastmilk much as it is in the blood, meaning that the milk in your body, if you leave it in there long enough and stop drinking, eventually will not have any alcohol in it. Pumping all of that milk out does not speed up the exit of that alcohol from your body.

In other words, the only reason to pump and dump after drinking alcohol is if you are super uncomfortable and need to get rid of the milk *now*. On top of this, less than two percent of alcohol in your body reaches your milk, so for a drink here or there, we are talking about a miniscule quantity.

The more relaxed approach, then, simply says that if I can feel the alcohol, my milk still has it, so I shouldn't nurse, and if I pump while I feel that way, the milk has got to go.

The most conservative route (next to never drinking while breastfeeding) is to follow stricter guidelines:
- Wait at least two hours after a drink before nursing (La Leche League and others say that alcohol in mother's milk peaks at 30 to 90 minutes after consumption).

- Have a drink *while* nursing or pumping. While this sounds incredibly boozy, it's actually conservative advice because it takes a while for alcohol to reach your bloodstream.
- Purchase test strips (Milkscreen is a leading brand) to test the alcohol content of any pumped milk. Just know that these turn positive with very low amounts of alcohol.

This drinking talk has to be tempered with the knowledge that some studies show that alcohol can hurt milk production and milk letdown. If you drink on occasion, keep an eye on these things. And now, it's up to you and your comfort level.

And, by the way: Coffee? Yes. I drink it. Moderate caffeine intake is fine. And if you're a working mom, I wouldn't dare try to take it away from you.

You Discover That Breastfeeding Is Difficult

Ever notice that the experts seem to be pretending this stuff is not difficult? I was so frustrated when I realized that not one of my stack of pregnancy and nursing books had told me that my nipples would probably bleed. I was frustrated when I had my first (of many, oh, so many) awkward encounters about pumping at work, and felt totally unprepared for it. I was frustrated when I almost lost my mind with anxiety because of the pressure I was putting on myself to "make it" to a year of breastfeeding with my first child (reminder: I didn't make it).

So while this book is technically about pumping and working, I would be remiss if I didn't take a few lines to just tell you that breastfeeding, in any form, is hard work. It's often physically painful for the first days or weeks, and that doesn't always mean a tongue tie or bad latch. (If the pain persists or gets worse, even if you were told you had a good latch, seek out your trusty lactation professional.)

It's time-consuming. Don't let anyone tell you it's "free"—your time has worth! And it's often anxiety-inducing if you're the goal-oriented type who puts pressure on herself to achieve.

It's also great in many ways, for most women. It's sweet and snuggly and something only you can give. But for all of its benefits to you and to your baby, for all of the sweet moments it can offer, it is also exhausting to loan your body out day in and day out, and it's okay to recognize that. Adding working and pumping on top of this just makes it harder.

Breastfeeding. Is. Really. Hard.

There, I said it, because somebody needs to say it. I hope that just saying it will help you meet your own breastfeeding goals more successfully, because I don't think the truth will make you run screaming from trying.

You Hate Breastfeeding

It's so natural! It's ecstasy-inducing! The bond with my baby is amazing! I love breastfeeding!

. . . Unless you don't. More women than you might suspect just tolerate it or even outright hate it.

Kelly had a really hard time with breastfeeding pain, and asked, "What bonding? Breastfeeding is the equivalent of putting clothespins on my nipples for forty minutes, ten times a day." She also told me, "The day I decided to quit breastfeeding, I immediately felt less resentful and more happy about being a parent. I even tried cabbage on my boobs because they hurt so bad. Now I can't eat cabbage without thinking about breastfeeding. I love my child dearly, but she has ruined stir fry for me forever."

The fact is, for some women, breastfeeding ranges from painful to annoying to plain old boring. It's "free," except it is an enormous drain (pardon the pun) on the mother, who is responsible for all of the baby's nutrition around the clock. It's "natural," but so are fire ant bites and those hurt like the devil.

Your baby's milk does not have any fewer wonderful qualities because you hate producing it. A newborn feels no less cozy while nursing just because you happen to be watching TV because you are bored to tears. If this is you but you want to breastfeed (or pump) anyway, please cut yourself loose from the guilt that you don't like it.

You Wonder What Co-Workers Think

Pumping can create a lot of time for obsessive thinking. A favorite topic of working mothers is what others think we're doing in there. Every time you have to step out of a meeting early, you can go into a spiral of wondering if everyone is picturing you pumping (they're not, because unless they have kids, they have no idea what it entails), wondering if they all roll their eyes behind your back every time you leave (they might, if they're total jerks), and wondering if you are totally ruining your career by doing this.

I just want to put this in perspective: Most people are not thinking about you, I swear. People are too wrapped up in their own business to really spend much time on you. Also, you are doing this for a finite amount of time. In the grand scheme of things, this will be over in a heartbeat, and you'll be proud that you tried it.

You Get Pressure to Stop

Pressure to stop breastfeeding or pumping can be almost as intense as the pressure all around us to continue breastfeeding. Spouses, co-workers, mothers, and relatives—everyone seems to have an opinion. If you want to continue breastfeeding and start getting comments or direct "advice" to stop, you can arm yourself ahead of time with your responses so you're not caught off-guard and flustered. There is nothing worse than thinking of the best comeback ten minutes too late.

I present to you your starter kit of comebacks for these situations. Imagine someone saying to you, "You're *still* breastfeeding? Isn't it time you wrapped that up?" Your responses, from gentle to badass:

- "It's hard. But we're going to keep going a little longer."
- "Not just yet . . . but thank you for asking."
- "My doctor says it's great to keep going, so I'm doing my best."
- "Nah, I'm thinking if we just keep going for the next eighteen years, we'll save money by not needing to get him a meal plan in college."
- "What, and give up the free 500 calories a day?"
- "I'll get right on it. Now, let's talk about *your* boobs."
- "I can't believe you're trying to have this conversation with me. This is so completely inappropriate."
- "I would, but what would my husband put in his coffee?"

You Get Grief That You Did Stop

Because nothing about parenting is simple, there will also be those in your life who give you hell for "giving up" breastfeeding. Again, from gentle to badass, you might consider saying:

- "It was hard for me, so thanks for asking how I'm doing."
- "I can't believe Child Protective Services hasn't shown up yet."
- "I can't think of anything that is less your business."

You Can't (or Don't Want to) Work a Full Week

For many women, a change in job just isn't possible—or, equally valid, isn't something they want to do.

If you find yourself really struggling with making your job work with breastfeeding, you could consider alternative work scenarios, if your employer and financial situation allow for it.

Some women are able to work out temporary changes: going part-time, job sharing, telecommuting for part of the day or for whole days, or a shortened/compressed week in which you work longer hours over fewer days. Bringing these ideas to your boss and HR require much of the same planning as seen in Chapter 8.

Ask yourself the same kinds of questions: What will make them confident in your ability to do this? What kind of personalities are you dealing with? What's the business case? What drawbacks will this scenario have, and how will you address them? Tone remains important: you are not begging, but you are also not "owed" this. Build as strong a case as possible and present it confidently.

You Feel Totally "Touched Out"

I love my kids. I feel I need to state that up front in case what follows seems to contradict that incontrovertible fact.

Sometimes I don't want them to touch me. There are times when I think I'll take leave of my sanity if someone touches me.

Breastfeeding (and pumping, in its own way) is so much physical touching, which everyone says is supposed to be wonderful. It sometimes is, but it is just as often tedious, and it is sometimes even overwhelming.

Feeling "touched out" is totally normal, and I'm here to ask you not to feel bad about it. When it gets really bad for me, I either ask my husband for a hall pass to leave the house for a while, or I just set the kitchen timer on the oven for ten minutes, announce that no one is to touch me until the timer goes off (if they do, it gets reset to ten minutes again), and go into my room with a book. Sometimes you just need a little breather and the reminder that you are allowed to set some boundaries around your body.

Chapter 18:
Stress and Guilt

A Short Story That Is Not Technically About Breastfeeding

My friend Anne had her baby girl within a week of my son's birth. When Anne's baby was a few weeks old, she and her husband took the baby to a Major League Baseball game, and Anne posted a photo of the three of them on Facebook. Eighteen months later, I was talking on the phone with Anne about breastfeeding and mom-guilt in general, and I mentioned that photo.

> Me: "Remember that photo you posted of you guys at the baseball game? It sent me into a shame spiral. I spent days thinking, 'Should we take our baby to a baseball game? Is he getting enough stimulation? They're such fun parents! I'm such a lame parent.'"

> Anne: "Oh. My. God. I posted that photo and spent days thinking, 'Should we not have taken her? There were so many germs there! It was so loud! My other friends would *never* do this! We're such bad parents.'"

In other words: Motherhood is the most efficient anxiety-and self-judgment delivery system I've ever found. And in new motherhood, breastfeeding is the turbo charger to that system.

I Blame Myself (Daily)

Generally speaking, we new mothers are horrible to ourselves. Why do we spend so many hours of the day analyzing our merit as mothers, talking ourselves off ledges, explaining to ourselves that we are doing okay at this, berating ourselves for what we didn't do today, and comparing ourselves to the impossibly high standards we assume of those mothers around us?

This state of mind seems to be especially true when it comes to breastfeeding. Yes, there are mothers who blissfully do, or do not, breastfeed, and don't seem to pay any mind to what is being said by society or their friends or their mothers or that horrible lady at the playground (if this is your first child, you haven't met her yet, but you will . . . oh, you will).

For the majority of women, guilt and self-judgment are part and parcel of breastfeeding. From "Am I making enough milk?" to "Is my milk nutritious enough?" to "I want/need to stop breastfeeding but isn't that selfish of me?" to "I just want a glass of wine," the road through breastfeeding is peppered with landmines of guilt.

In writing this book, I spent a lot of time thinking about why the typical mom-guilt factor seems to be on steroids when it comes to

Stress and Guilt

breastfeeding. There are a lot of reasons, but at the moment your baby is born, my theory goes like this:

A newborn baby is placed in your arms. You've spent the past nine-and-a-half months worrying about how you're going to keep this person alive. Everything you eat, every glass of wine you turn down or don't turn down, every time you wake up in the night to realize you've been sleeping on your back when your doctor told you not to, you have been basically the only person responsible for this baby.

Your maternal instincts are at an all-time high. Think being pregnant made you motherly? Pregnancy has nothing on the rush of hormones and instincts now flooding your brain and body. At this moment, you were built and made to protect this baby, whom you love more than you imagined possible (if you don't feel that feeling yet, don't add this to the Guilt List. It will kick in eventually, I promise). Women doing this successfully over the millennia is why we have a human race to speak of. The gazillions of women who came before you are all whispering into the tiny ears of each of your hyperactive hormones, "You're the last line of defense between this baby and sudden disaster."

For many women, this is our *only* job for the time being. In a baby's first weeks of life, we have nothing to judge ourselves on (and what would we do if we couldn't judge ourselves constantly?) other than our performance as mothers. No performance reviews, sales targets, budgets, or bonuses at work. No beating your best time on a five-mile-run (please don't try to do this in the first few weeks of your baby's life), no secretly looking around the yoga studio to compare your headstand to your classmates', no put-together outfit to feel accomplished about (just kind of cross that last one off your list for a good, long while). No hours of volunteer work in the community. No "how many beers can I chug in ten minutes?" (I'm not judging your pre-baby lifestyle.)

There are many things in our lives that normally give us satisfaction. They remind us that we are able to be our best, to set standards for ourselves and meet and exceed them. Almost all of them are on hold, except for being a mom to this baby. Naturally, this one thing takes on monumental importance.

So, there's your totally screwed up mental state. If this isn't you, I am so, so happy for you. Please come to my house and parent my children while I go out for a drink.

Milk, Stress, and the Working Mother

Now stir in a big dose of sleep deprivation and add going back to work into the mix. Not only does going back to work add to your exhaustion and deplete the time you have with your baby, it also introduces the element of juggling milk-making and bread-winning. Now, you can choose: Feel guilty about being away from baby? Or feel guilty about the fact that taking time to pump is hurting your productivity at work? How about both!

I asked hundreds of working mothers how trying to work and breastfeed made them feel. And it turns out the answer is: amazing and terrible at the same time. The majority of women I interviewed cited negative feelings like anxiety, stress, and guilt . . . as well as pride at juggling it all and producing milk for the baby and excitement to be back at work.

Some were candid about being annoyed that pumping was taking them away from diving back into work, and some felt guilty that they were glad to be at work and get a break from the baby.

All of them were exhausted at the dual demands of work and motherhood.

Some felt a lot of pressure from co-workers to stop breastfeeding—especially as they neared or passed the one-year mark. I was surprised at how much of this pressure seemed to come from female co-workers who made comments about formula being just fine for babies (it is, but that's not the point) or about the baby being "too old" for breastfeeding.

Many were surprised at their own answers, saying they hadn't realized just how mixed (and strong) their emotions about the whole thing were. As Julie remarked, "Nothing has ever made me feel so empowered and so inadequate at the same time."

The working/breastfeeding thing breeds its own catalog of things to stress about, feel guilty about, and get super self-judgmental about.

Wanting to Work

Some women love to work and get excited to go back after having a baby. They want to use their professional brain and skill set. They find non-stop time with a tiny person who can't talk and is very needy to be a little boring after a while. Some of these women feel horribly guilty about these feelings. To you I say: Stop it. You are doing something that fulfills you, and hopefully will continue to fulfill you long after your kids are off in college, doing keg stands and not calling you.

Obsessing Over Milk Supply

Obsessing over milk comes in many different forms, and it is especially bad for women who pump, because you can actually see and count the ounces of milk.

When my son was born, I developed a counting problem. At night, I would find myself visited by insomnia, and I would stand in front of the freezer and count up my ounces of precious milk. I regularly reported to anyone who would listen how much I had gotten up to in my stash (I was so very fun at parties).

While at work and on business trips, I kept a detailed list of how many ounces I was pumping, and made our caregivers keep an equally detailed log and report it to me daily via email, so I could see if I was producing more than my son was consuming. If I wasn't, I'd add an extra pumping session the next day. While this can be a good way to keep an eye on your supply, it got to a point of being unhealthy for me.

Getting obsessed with counting is a very real danger. And why wouldn't it be? In many ways, if you forget that whole "does she feel loved and safe" thing, you might be tempted to define your success as a parent in your child's infancy by numbers only: ounces per feeding, minutes on each side while breastfeeding, ounces pumped, ounces of milk in the fridge or freezer, weight gained by the baby, wet diapers per day, hours of sleep, months of breastfeeding. There are just so damn many things to count, all of which feel very, very important at the time. For the controlling type, counting returns a sense of control to a pretty crazy situation.

If you're the counting type, there's no reason to pretend that you are just going to up and stop counting stuff. In fact, some counting is good. It's good to make sure your baby is getting enough to eat and gaining enough weight—but your pediatrician is there to help you with that. It's good to keep a rough count of diapers at the beginning, to be sure your baby is hydrated and fed. It's good to take note of how many ounces of breastmilk your spouse spilled so you can use the number to very specifically berate and hate him (kidding, kidding). Some basic counting is not our enemy.

Obsession with counting, on the other hand, is an issue to look out for. This might mean that you spend a lot of time in front of the freezer, like me. It might mean that you obsess silently over every feeding, wondering how many ounces your baby is getting. It could be that you keep terrifyingly detailed poop logs until your child's fifth birthday. Maybe you set a breastfeeding goal for yourself and move the goalposts out every time you reach it, and constantly ask other women how long they breastfed so you can secretly compare your progress to theirs.

If these things serve you, go with them. But I'd also gently suggest that you periodically ask yourself whether these things *actually* serve you or whether they just feed the beast. I'm not judging you, because boy have I been there. I'm just, as your friend through these pages, worried about you, and don't want you to get overwhelmed.

Postpartum Mood Disorders

Have I mentioned that pumping and working is hard? Yes, it can be incredibly rewarding and a way to feel connected to your baby while you're at work. But it's also yet another thing to keep in the front of your mind at all times—tallying up ounces and minutes and washing and storing and where am I going to pump and will this meeting end in time for me to pump and oh no I forgot milk storage bags. It feeds into what we're already doing to ourselves: putting pressure and judgment on ourselves and allowing others to put pressure and judgment on us. And sometimes all of that anxiety and worry can get out of hand.

I want to talk about postpartum mood disorders briefly, so you can try to recognize them if or when you see them. You probably have heard about postpartum depression (PPD) and its symptoms. You often hear about women being listless, not interested in the baby, and crying all the time. Watch for these signs in yourself and in your fellow mom-warriors.

But while PPD gets a lot of attention, PPD's cousin, postpartum anxiety (PPA) is also a thing, and it can look very different. PPA can look like worrying excessively, not being able to sleep, and so many other things. PPD, too, can look like being angry or having mood swings, and so many other things. There's are a lot of symptoms that don't get talked about in popular culture.

You could, like me with my first child, find yourself *over*-interested in the baby and totally unable to imagine how you would be able to go back to work and leave the baby for one second. I was wracked with anxiety as a result of these thoughts. I didn't fit the PPD profile at all, so it took me a while to figure out that I needed some help.

There are also other PMADs (perinatal mood and anxiety disorders), like postpartum OCD, post-traumatic stress syndrome, and postpartum psychosis. I don't provide this list to scare you, just to let you know that the stereotypical PPD that we all hear about is only a slice of postpartum mood disorders.

Please, please seek professional help if you have even the slightest inclination that your situation may be moving beyond "sucky but normal" into "not so normal" territory. You don't have to go the pharmaceutical route (I know women who have benefited from it, but I am not one of those women), but you do need to reach out and start the conversation.

It can be really scary to say the words "postpartum" *anything* to anybody. I remember worrying that if I said those words to my husband, he would assume I was on the verge of hurting myself or the baby (which I wasn't, but those thoughts can happen too). That worry alone almost stopped me from speaking up. Sometimes you just don't want to say it out loud because you don't want it to be true.

Secrecy is fertilizer for postpartum issues. If you don't want it to get really true, really fast, just *say* something. And if the first person you say something to doesn't pay attention—be it your spouse, a friend, or your OB/GYN—find someone else. Keep saying it until someone starts to listen.

Pick up the phone or write an email, for starters, and reach out to a mom friend. She may seem like she has it all together, but I can guarantee you she's been there in one way or another. Tell her, in gory detail, how off-kilter you are thinking or acting right now. Nothing can shock this woman if she has had a baby. She will tell you her own stories that will curl your hair, and she will make you feel like it's okay to talk about your anxiety and stress and exhaustion and frustration.

Regardless of whether you think you are at risk of postpartum mood issues, connected to breastfeeding or not, you can also put some safeguards in place before the baby even arrives.

I formed a small committee of mom-friends before my second child was born and charged them with regularly checking in on my mental state. These women, and my husband, were true to their word, asking me probing questions about my mental state. They were ruthless in their questioning because I made them promise they would be.

Take care of yourself, and each other. Motherhood is powerful stuff, and that is mostly amazing, but there can be a dark side to that power, and we owe it to each other to keep each other in good health.

We Are With You

As you head off to climb this big old mountain, I just want to ask you to do one more thing: Picture us, your army of fellow working mothers, who love you.

We are out there too, feeling guilty and proud all at once.

We are sitting with you, pump perched precariously on your knees, typing an email on your phone, in the storage closet.

We are running with you across the office or the school or the courthouse or the hospital building, late for a meeting but needing to get that milk into the fridge that is located about as far away from the lactation room as it can get.

We are experiencing that moment of nausea with you when you spill breastmilk all over your keyboard (tell IT that it was coffee).

We are with you as your heart sinks when you get to work and realize you only brought half of your pump parts.

We are cheering with you when you make it to a breastfeeding milestone you never thought you'd reach.

We are sharing that quiet moment with you every evening when you fill up your baby's bottles with whatever you're feeding him, ready for the next day.

We are with you at the store when you buy your first canister of formula, and you cry in the aisle. And we are with you when your baby drinks that formula; we are whispering in your ear that this is okay, this is good, you are still the same good mother you were yesterday.

We are raising a glass of wine to you when the kids are in bed, in that blissful five minutes before one of them starts crying again.

We are so, so proud of you for being a working mom and for giving this breastfeeding and working thing a shot. And we're just dying to hear *your* war stories and successes in this journey.

So Go Already

Now get out there, attach a machine to one of the most sensitive and private parts of your body, and make the magic happen.

You're a warrior. You're a badass. You're a working mother, and that's an amazing thing.

And when you see one of us on the street, at the airport, or on the train (you'll know us by our "this is supposed to look like a briefcase" pump bag), know that we are on your side. We're exhausted. We have dried breastmilk on our work pants. We have pumped in places we never imagined possible. And we think you're awesome.

Chapter 19: Resources

If you're looking for me, you can find me online, where I write about modern parenthood, breastfeeding, and more.

Information on this book and related content are at www.workpumprepeat.com. You can also find me on Facebook at www.facebook.com/JessicaShortallWrites and blogging at www.italkaboutboobs.wordpress.com. On twitter, I use the handle @PumpatWork for the obvious and @JessicaShortall for a little bit of everything. I also do some public speaking (keynotes, commencement addresses, workshops, and seminars) on the topics of changing the world, women and girls, leadership, and of course, modern motherhood. You can find more on my public speaking and other day job stuff at www.jessicashortall.com.

Most of the resources in this chapter can be found online. Active and reputable organizations maintain and update their information as laws and circumstances change. Where web links are lengthy, I have also included key words to use in a Google search should the address not work for you.

Legal Rights

United States Breastfeeding Committee

- Federal and state laws about working and breastfeeding
- Campaigns to change state and federal law
- www.usbreastfeeding.org

National Conference of State Legislatures

- Comprehensive list of state laws on breastfeeding
- www.ncsl.org/research/health/breastfeeding-state-laws.aspx
- Google search: NCSL breastfeeding

United States Department of Labor

- Information and links to fact sheets and resources
- www.dol.gov/whd/nursingmothers
- Google search: DOL break time nursing mothers

Making Changes at Your Workplace

Centers for Disease Control and Prevention

- Lactation Support Program has a toolkit for creating a lactation support program at work
- www.cdc.gov/nccdphp/dnpao/hwi/toolkits/lactation
- Google search: CDC lactation support program

Resources

Womenshealth.gov

- See "Government in action" under "Breastfeeding resources" section for the business case for breastfeeding
- www.womenshealth.gov/breastfeeding
- Google search: Office Women's Health business case breastfeeding

Choosing a Breast Pump

USDA

- WIC covers some pumps for women who qualify for assistance. WIC is administered state-by-state, and every state WIC office has its own website. If you can't find information online, call the office and ask.
- www.fns.usda.gov/wic/women-infants-and-children-wic for list of state agency contact information, including a link for breastfeeding coordinators in each state.
- Google search: (state name) WIC breastfeeding

Online reviews of breast pumps

- www.consumerreports.org/cro/breast-pumps/buying-guide.htm
- www.breastpumpcomparisons.com
- Check out Amazon reviews of various pumps

Breastfeeding and Travel

Transportation Safety Authority (USA)

- TSA is the body that manages airport security in the U.S. Their website is vague on the detailed points about traveling with a pump and milk, but the link below is worth printing and bringing with you.
- www.tsa.gov/traveling-formula-breast-milk-and-juice
- Google search: TSA breastmilk

General Breastfeeding Support

To make sense of the landscape of lactation support available, I enlisted the help of Robyn Roche-Paull, BSN, RN, IBCLC. Robyn is the author of *Breastfeeding in Combat Boots*, and a former Navy mechanic, so she is also a certified badass. Here's Robyn:

"An IBCLC, also known as a lactation consultant, has received the highest level of education and training and has the knowledge and skill to help mothers with even the most difficult breastfeeding situations.

"To use the letters IBCLC, one must pass a rigorous international exam. To be eligible to sit for the exam she must have extensive education (usually a four-year degree) and thousands of hours of experience with breastfeeding mothers. To retain the credential, she must attend conferences and earn continuing education credits. IBCLCs often have an area of expertise (such as working mothers or cleft palate babies), and charge for their services.

"Certified lactation counselors or educators (CLC or CLE) have taken one or more short-term breastfeeding courses and may have a local or national certification. CLCs are capable of teaching mothers about breastfeeding and helping with normal problems, but may or may not have the expertise to help with difficult problems.

"Breastfeeding USA counselors and La Leche League Leaders are mothers who have breastfed for at least nine months to a year and completed a lengthy accreditation process with extensive coursework. Both are volunteers who provide peer support by facilitating monthly support group meetings and offer breastfeeding counseling via telephone and email support.

"WIC Peer Counselors are mothers who are or have been on the WIC Program and have breastfed. They receive extensive training and provide peer counseling, and can often help with normal breastfeeding problems."

Breastfeeding in Combat Boots: A Survival Guide to Successful Breastfeeding While Serving in the Military
- Robyn Roche-Paull's awesome book for military moms is also great for firefighters, law enforcement, EMTs, and anyone pulling long, physical shifts outside of an office setting.
- www.breastfeedingincombatboots.com

For online breastfeeding support, try the following resources:

Kellymom.com
- Advice on common breastfeeding issues
- Medication safety while pregnant and breastfeeding
- www.kellymom.com

La Leche League International
- Directory of local La Leche League support groups
- Resources for many common breastfeeding concerns
- www.llli.org

Directories of Lactation Consultants
- Global directory of IBCLCs: www.ilca.org
- U.S. directory of lactation consultants: www.uslca.org

Breastfeeding USA
- Articles and resources for working moms
- www.breastfeedingusa.org

LowMilkSupply.org
- Lactation-consultant-run website with help for low supply
- www.lowmilksupply.org

Apps

This list is not comprehensive, but these apps might be especially useful to a working breastfeeder:

- Breastfeeding Solutions: practical advice from an IBCLC
- Pacify: on-demand advice from lactation experts
- LactMed: information about drugs and breastfeeding
- iLetDown: baby crying sounds to help with letdown (you could also record your baby crying on your own phone)
- Pump@work: tracks daily milk and storage totals
- Milk Maid: tracks pumping time, output, and how much stash you have in different locations.
- Breastfeeding Central: IBCLC answers to questions, and a locator to find lactation professionals

Made in the USA
Charleston, SC
23 December 2014